Praise for *Stepford Daughters*

T0028654

"In this brilliant and compulsively readable book, Johan[ ]
recent horror films, focusing on what they tell us about [ ]
films in the 21st century are a kind of social realism. They hold a mirror up to social conditions that are so ubiquitous and so commonly taken for granted, that we have forgotten that we can fight back against them. Isaacson shows us how horror films can work as tools for understanding, and even for social transformation." —**Steven Shaviro**, DeRoy Professor of English, Wayne State University

"Johanna Isaacson is a worthy successor to Robin Wood and Carol Clover, and *Stepford Daughters* deftly analyzes some of the most popular and accomplished contemporary horror films at the nexus of feminism and capitalism. Full of brilliant insights that apply decades of feminist theory to horror cinema, this is essential reading for horror scholars, pop culture enthusiasts, and anyone who desires a greater insight into the intersectional dynamics of the capitalist class war." —**Michael Truscello**, author of *Infrastructural Brutalism: Art and the Necropolitics of Infrastructure*

"Johanna Isaacson's *Stepford Daughters* is a brilliant and critically important elucidation of how 'class horror is gender horror' in the twenty-first century. The book explores twenty contemporary horror films that depict how public and private, work and family, have become intertwined under neoliberal politics—and how labor at home and in the workplace has become increasingly feminized and devalued. With an incisive theoretical framework and incredibly rich and illuminating readings, Isaacson's book offers a much-needed approach to horror, eloquently demonstrating how horror films can both diagnose the problems of neoliberal and gendered capitalism and give us monstrous figures who resist and transform." —**Dawn Keetley,** editor of *Jordan Peele's Get Out: Political Horror*

"Surveying dozens of recent horror films and engaging a rich critical archive of social reproduction theory, *Stepford Daughters* makes provocative and evocative interventions into contemporary cultural theory. A leading scholar in the field of horror criticism whose work is also broadly accessible, Isaacson offers readings that are at once militant and playful, and she persuasively locates in the horror genre a radical current of Marxist-feminist critique that we need now more than ever." —**Annie McClanahan**, author of *Dead Pledges: Debt, Crisis, and Twenty-First-Century Culture*

"Johanna Isaacson's *Stepford Daughters* draws from social reproduction to explore the way in which contemporary horror illustrates the intimacy of exploitation. It proposes not just a new understanding of recent horror films, but a groundbreaking illustration of the monstrosity of daily life under contemporary capitalism, colonialism, and patriarchy." —**Jason Read,** author of *The Production of Subjectivity: Marx and Philosophy*

ISBN: 978-1-942173-69-4 | eBook ISBN: 978-1-942173-67-0
Library of Congress Number: 2022934106

10 9 8 7 6 5 4 3 2 1

Common Notions
c/o Interference Archive
314 7th St.
Brooklyn, NY 11215

Common Notions
c/o Making Worlds Bookstore
210 S. 45th St.
Philadelphia, PA 19104

www.commonnotions.org
info@commonnotions.org

Discounted bulk quantities of our books are available for organizing, educational, or fundraising purposes. Please contact Common Notions at the addresses above for more information.

Cover design by Josh MacPhee
Layout design and typesetting by Graciela "Chela" Vasquez / ChelitasDesign

Printed by union labor in Canada on acid-free paper

Stepford Daughters

Stepford Daughters

Weapons for Feminists in Contemporary Horror

Johanna Isaacson

Brooklyn, NY
Philadelphia, PA
commonnotions.org

CONTENTS

Acknowledgments   *v*

Introduction: Class Horror Is Gender Horror   1

Chapter 1: It's Coming from Inside/Outside the House:
Horror as Care Strike   29

Hereditary (2018)
The Babadook (2014)
Under the Shadow (2016)
Dark Water (2002)
The Happiness of the Katakuris (2001)

Chapter 2: It's Coming from Inside the Boss's House:
Horror and Waged Domestic Work   67

Housekeeping (2015)
The Maid (2005)
Get Out (2017)
La Llorona (2019)
Good Manners (2017)

Chapter 3: The Telltale Managed Heart:
Service Labor and Emotional Labor in Contemporary Horror   105

Maps to the Stars (2014)
Parasite (2019)
I Blame Society (2020)
Cam (2018)
Sorry to Bother You (2018)

Chapter 4: Coming of Rage:
Teens Entering the Futureless Future in Contemporary Horror   145

It Follows (2014)
Assassination Nation (2018)
The Fits (2015)
The Lure (2015)
Teeth (2007)

Coda: Becoming Monster   183

About the Author   189

Acknowledgements

Thanks so much to Andy Battle, Hunter Bivens, Nicki Kattoura, Madeline Lane-McKinley, Marsh Leicester, and Kenan Sharpe for invaluable editorial help, and to Common Notions Press for their comradely support.

I am so grateful to my family and friends, my amazing horror watching group, my colleagues and students at MJC, my "Love Boat" mutual aid crew, the professors and peers who helped me through grad school in UCSC's Literature department, the Marxist Literary Group, Red May, my coeditors and contributors to *Blind Field*, and all the folks who chat with me in real life and on social media about horror and politics. Everything good in this book and in my life is because of you!

Dedicated to Finn Bivens, the feminist future!

Introduction

CLASS HORROR IS GENDER HORROR

You think you know this story. You think it's the story your mother told you. An ambitious woman with hopes and dreams is submerged in a nightmare. She is trapped in her home, reduced to nothing but a caregiver. You think it's the story of Joanna from the 1975 film *The Stepford Wives*. Joanna was smart and educated. She loved photography and dirty jokes. But once she moves to Stepford, her husband joins a "men's society" that has a plan for unruly spouses: to turn them into robot housewives, content with a friendless, jobless life of chores and husbands, dust and dirt.

Forty-two years later, another woman, Amelia, is trapped in a suburban house with her difficult son. By day, she tries to keep it together and at night a cadaverous spectral monster stalks her dreams. She becomes increasingly dissociated—her mind drifts darkly as she washes the dishes and cleans the house. In the kitchen she finds a slit in the wall pouring out cockroaches. Later, as she lies sleepless at night, an ominous shadow spreads across the ceiling, suddenly flying into her petrified, screaming mouth. After this, she will no longer be an exhausted mother, but the powerful, murderous Babadook, ready to slaughter her own child to get back the husband she has lost.

Like Joanna, Amelia is driven to horrific extremes by domestic life. Some things never change. And yet, things have changed. Joanna was depicted as a victim of what Betty Friedan called "the problem with no name," entrapment in the home.[1] You can see women afflicted with this unutterable difficulty march in lockstep: the robotic Stepford Wives in their

---

1 Betty Friedan, *The Feminine Mystique* (New York: Norton, 2001).

matching aprons, plastered smiles, obsessing over their cleaning products, having relinquished all aspirations and independence. The cure prescribed to them was to get out of their suburban homes and into the job market.

This is not the way out for our single working mom, Amelia. She suffers the demeaning horrors of domestic life, but her terrors don't stop at the threshold of the home. Inside and outside her gloomy house she is stretched to the max, working a precarious job as a caretaker in an old-age home where abandoned elders clamor for her constant emotional labor. The work world has not solved her problems but has compounded them. As the pressures overtake her, building to her demonic possession, she calls in sick to work. In response, all her shifts are taken away, leaving Amelia's future even more uncertain and strained. It is only then, when the total weight of this merciless world is bearing down on her, that she fully transforms into the monster.

In thinking about the transition from *The Stepford Wives* to *The Babadook* we can look back to classic horror films that captured their audiences by building a genealogy, or line of descent. In the thirties we encounter such titles as *Son of Frankenstein* and *Dracula's Daughter* that built on the popularity of name-recognition monsters. While this is no longer the style, horror films are still adept at forming critical lineages. There is a continuous thread of feminist critique throughout the history of horror, but the terms of this criticism mutate to suit changing realities.

In this sense, Amelia is, like other feminized people of horror discussed in this book, a "Stepford Daughter." By this, I mean that the women of contemporary horror, and of the present world at large, have inherited the oppressive conditions of the housewife but are examples of how these problems historically transform. We don't want to forget what our mothers struggled for (and against). As we face a bleak neoliberal world of austerity and precarity, however, we need to know how gendered oppression works *now*.

Stepford Daughters

As I imagine Amelia's backstory, I see her growing up in the suburbs, tended by a zombified mother, zoned out on Quaaludes (mother's "little helpers") and living to find the shiniest brand of floor wax. Or maybe she really did grow up in (the Australian version of) Stepford and her mother, like the characters in the film, was a creative, vibrant second-wave feminist who was literally turned into a robot to suit her husband's desire for a compliant and constantly sexually available wife.

Either way, young Amelia is determined not to turn into this zombie-progenitor. Like many women of my generation (X), she has great dreams that must be modified as the realities of capitalism crash in. She first decides to become a doctor, but when she sees the student loans and years of impoverished apprenticeship stretch out before her, she decides to think again. Then she resolves to be independent, but facing a world that offers only the couple-form or abject loneliness, she concedes that she probably should get married. Still, this marriage won't be like her mother's, she'll at least work part time. Her job will be meaningful, helping elders in a nursing home. At first, she is thrilled to be able to help others and get paid at the same time but she soon discovers that the facility where she works pushes this caring instinct to its limits. Understaffed and underequipped, it leaves her little time and energy to care for her wards, let alone her own household. Now, however, she finds she can't afford to quit. The "family wage" that enabled a man to support his wife and kids is a thing of the past, and even households with two incomes can't keep up. Welcome to the life of the new, liberated woman!

We enter Amelia's life after she has lost her husband and find her struggling to care for a son with special needs. Where she searches for social supports—personalized education and mental health help for herself and her son—she finds only judgement and rejection. As a Stepford Daughter, Amelia is devalued for the same reasons as her mother was—her feminized labor is seen as both worthless and "natural." But unlike her mother, she is no longer trapped in her middle-class house and nuclear family. Instead, she is set adrift in a sea of poverty and precarity, living a life that soon will become a horror film. This is the endgame of a society that both relies on and disavows social reproduction.

The Babadook is just one example of a canny new wave of horror films exploring the dark side of phenomena we typically associate with patriarchy, such as women's confinement to the home, domestic labor, the pressures to look beautiful and young, the compulsion to be the perfect mother, the demand to be emotionally supportive while ignoring one's own needs, the fear of sexual assault.

The twist to these films is that they show how these traditional feminist concerns are linked to capitalism as a whole. In *American Mary*, a woman achieves revenge against her rapist *and* defeats her student loans. In *Maps to the Stars*, a young woman destroys her abusive family unit *and* kills her boss. In *Unfriended*, the ghost of a girl driven to suicide by sexist bullying destroys her tormentors *and* social media. And in all of these cases, the films show how there is no way to separate gendered oppression from capitalist oppression.

Why look to horror films to understand the linked oppressions of heteropatriarchy and capitalism? Don't get me wrong, horror films can be sexist and conservative. In addition to the piled-up bodies of dead, naked women that cater to violent misogynist fantasies, horror can serve as a retrograde force that warns us what will happen if we don't behave. Barry Grant gives the example of Tod Browning's *Dracula*, in which we are told to be terrified of Dracula's unleashed sexuality. By depicting untamed, excessive desire as evil, Browning is warning us that if we don't retreat to Victorian sex-negative repression, we too will become victims, monsters, or both. While I don't entirely agree with Grant's interpretation of the film, this reading shows how fear can be disciplinary.[2]

But there is a flip side to horror, a genre that explores taboo topics. In this book I seek out films that explore forbidden forms of *realism*, accurately showing the horrors of contemporary social forms and unleashing dark, but ultimately utopian fantasies of fighting back. Commercial, middle-brow genres avoid depicting these realities, as exposing the myths that secure contemporary power relations threatens those who benefit from those myths' proliferation and invisibility. But for most of us, speaking the truth, even if it horrific, is therapeutic, if not revolutionary. We may emerge from the experience of watching these films breathless or even nauseated—and these emotions are entirely appropriate for the horrors we see represented—but seeing

---

2 Barry Keith Grant, "Screams on Screens: Paradigms of Horror," *Loading: The Journal of the Canadan Game Studies Association* 4, no. 6, (2010).

these terrors on the screen (rather than tucked under the bed or hidden in the closet) can also help us feel seen and heard.

Marxism and Feminism Together

In this book I am going to concentrate on the ways that horror films help us understand that the *exploitation of social reproduction* makes the capitalist system possible. By social reproduction I am referring to tasks, emotions, and behaviors that seem to be the "natural" domain of women. These activities are essential to our survival, but are dismissed as trivial and worthless, partially because of a historically sexist culture that degrades everything labeled "feminine." While this question has rarely been explored in horror criticism, looking at horror films through Marxist and feminist theory is not new. In the book *Pretend We're Dead*, Annalee Newitz elaborates the prevalence of "capitalist monsters" in today's horror films. And Barbara Creed's *The Monstrous Feminine* makes the convincing case that fear and disgust of women haunts the deepest recesses of the genre. These are just two of many books and articles that have plumbed the politics of horror film. But the two theories are often applied separately, as if capitalism and patriarchy are two distinct monsters.

In the past, horror criticism often fell into separate Marxist and feminist camps. *Either* we see vampires as blood sucking capitalists *or* as lesbian avengers. Frankenstein's monster is *either* an oppressed proletarian worker *or* a queer outcast searching for a friend. In some films, however, the connections are impossible to ignore. For example, *The Shining's* Jack Torrance is a patriarchal monster who terrorizes his family, but it is evident that his own economic immiseration drives him to these extremes. More connections can be made. Frankenstein's monster is not *either* a worker *or* a queer outcast, he is an index of the fact that the unruly worker is always also violating heteronormativity. The lesbian vampires of films like *The Hunger* illustrate how capitalism only offers women the freedom to explore their desires if they agree to "lean in" to capitalism's predatory logic. In other words, if gender and capitalism overlap in the real world, why wouldn't they do so in the films that represent and process that world?

The problem of understanding the relationship of Marxism and feminism has a long and complicated history. In 1979 Heidi Hartmann famously published an article titled "The Unhappy Marriage of Marxism and Feminism," making the case that Marxism and feminism are separate "dual systems" that we must relate to each other. If we don't think carefully about it, we can imagine that Marxism—the study of political economy, the history of work, and class struggle—is a separate phenomenon from feminism—the study of gender relations and patriarchal oppression. However, the concept of social reproduction and other Marxist-feminist theories help us understand that *class oppression and gender oppression must be analyzed as one system*. The advantages of social reproduction as a way to reevaluate capitalism are outlined succinctly by Salar Mohandesi and Emma Teitelman. As they put it:

> Shifting our perspective from the point of production to that of social reproduction does not merely add to the narrative; it has the potential to transform that story. It allows us a far more nuanced approach to formation, one that focuses not simply on waged factory workers but on the articulation of different kinds of struggles—those of the waged and unwaged, men and women, whites and nonwhites, and citizens and immigrants. It allows us to deepen our understanding of the capitalist mode of production by showing how its rise was partly based on the manifold subsumption of socially reproductive activities under capitalist relations. Last, it allows us to approach the state in a more complex manner, revealing the crucial role that contests over social reproduction played in the historical formation of the state and its relationship to capitalists.[3]

Social reproduction, that which is seen by some as *separate* from work and the domain of "productive" activity, is actually a central

---

3 Salar Mohandesi and Emma Teitelman, "Without Reserves," in *Social Reproduction Theory: Remapping Class, Recentering Oppression*, edited by Tithi Bhattacharya (London: Pluto Press, 2017), 38.

battleground for our lives. Any attempt to make a clear distinction between class and gender oppression ignores the continuity and inter-dependence of productive and reproductive labor.

The representation of Amelia's life in *The Babadook* eloquently cuts through many of the myths that separate Marxism and feminism. Amelia's transformation into the Babadook is a response to her oppressive life, but we can't comprehend the ways Amelia is oppressed without understanding her relationship to feminized labor, precarity, social reproduction, and care.

Again, by *feminized labor* I refer to work that conforms to traits and activities that are traditionally seen as feminine—such as emotional expression, caring, and domestic chores. *Precarity*—a state of living and working that involves lack of security and low or no wages—comes about as the number of jobs and ways of living that conform to feminine traits expand. The low pay and insecurity of today's precarious jobs are justified by centuries of gendered conditioning. Feminized work is seen to be natural, of low value, and low skilled. Feminized laborers have traditionally been forced to do this work for free. So, goes the logic of capital, these workers should feel grateful to even be paid and employed at all. Asking for security and fair wages is simply greed. And yet, these jobs are arguably the most essential part of our culture. The feeding, caring for, and education of the general population constitutes their *social reproduction*. And without this work of social reproduction nothing else could exist. There could be no production, no profit, and no commodities without society, and there can be no society without social reproduction.

Imagine a factory worker who typically arrives at work with crisp overalls, a full lunch box, and an anticipation of returning to a home at the end of the day where he will be fed, play with his children, watch television, and have sex. All of this motivates him through his eight hours of drudgery. Without the *social reproduction* that sustains him, his workday would be a horror movie. He would arrive naked and starving, he would never be able to leave the workplace because he wouldn't have anywhere to go. Capital would have to find increasingly unsustainable ways to force him to labor. In the horror film

Sorry to Bother You this lack of social reproduction leads to a scenario where reluctant workers are converted into enslaved horse-people. But even these monsters find ways to revolt.

Lean Out Horror

The fact is, we live in a world in which capitalism preys on age-old stereotypes about feminine activity. "Women's work" is seen as trivial and low-skilled, and this allows it to be ignored or poorly paid. The middle-class strains of second-wave feminism that shaped the logic of *The Stepford Wives* held out the hope that women's entry into the waged-work world would be a moment of emancipation, but that was not at all the outcome. Instead, the jobs that women entered into—service labor, flexible labor, affective labor—were both expanded and degraded. It is no accident that in this moment when the majority of employment growth is in "service" professions (that now employ up to 80 percent of the workforce), wages have dropped, and, with the exponential growth of professions done in the home, women, and especially women of color, are more and more likely to be employed in jobs that are widely considered to be "abject" or even neo-feudal.[4]

At the same time that capitalism lures women into this low- or no-paid work, it disinvests from programs of social welfare, leading to what Nancy Fraser calls a "crisis of care."[5] The alternative offered to women is corporate "lean in" feminism in which, as Dawn Foster asserts, "there is no room for a civil life, a political life, an emotional life outside the nuclear family unit."[6] "Lean in" feminism, a term coined by Sheryl Sandberg, the Chief Operating Officer of Facebook, is, as Cinzia Arruzza, Tithi Battacharya, and Nancy Fraser insist, "a handmaiden of capitalism." This is ultimately a vision where ruling-class men and women share the task of managing exploitation.[7] It puts the burden on individual women to climb to the top,

4 Jason Smith, "Nowhere to Go: Automation Then and Now, Part Two," *Brooklyn Rail*, April 2017, https://brooklynrail.org/2017/04/field-notes/ Nowhere-to-Go-Automation-Then-and-Now-Part-Two.

5 Nancy Fraser, "Contradictions of Capital and Care," *New Left Review* 100, (July–Aug, 2016).

6 Dawn Foster, *Lean Out* (London: Repeater Press, 2015), 16.

7 Cinzia Arruzza, Tithi Battacharya, and Nancy Fraser, *Feminism for the 99%* (New York: Verso Books, 2019), 2–3.

necessitating leaving the majority of women behind, or rather, necessarily relying on the unremunerated social reproduction of their hyperexploited "sisters." These economically precarious, mostly non-white women are used as the means to free up time and unleash career-driven women's boundless individualistic ambition.

I find this "lean in" logic particularly galling in my work as a community college teacher in the Central Valley, one of California's most disadvantaged areas. A popular strain of pedagogy emphasizes teaching personal responsibility rather than focusing on the structural failures of our economic system. While I do feel that grit, resilience, and determination are important, it breaks my heart to think that if my students don't achieve their goals they will blame their own personal failings or their own lack of "grit." I write this after having to move all of my classes online during the coronavirus. My students are overwhelmed, struggling, questioning, and doubting themselves. One student completed the class from a hospital bed, another handwrote and mailed me his assignments because he had neither internet nor a computer, a third broke down and gave up in the face of having to care for and homeschool her three small children full time, a fourth became the only breadwinner in the family as both his parents lost their jobs. This leaves me to ask, is it grit or structural change that these students need? The answer is clear, but it is also obscured everywhere. What I want to say to my students is that this optimistic ideal of a meritocratic world is for many, like the sun-soaked Swedish meadows in the horror film *Midsommar*, a cult. It's rigged. And as we've seen from the response to the coronavirus, this cult will kill your elders, as well as your young.

Contemporary horror has recognized the monstrosity of this logic of grit and "lean in," especially in the brilliant work of South Korean director Bong Joon-ho. In his film *Snowpiercer* the world has come to a halt due to global warming, and the only survivors live on a circumnavigational train in which classes are segregated by separate cars. Tilda Swinton, costumed to resemble Margaret Thatcher, plays Minister Mason, one of the most powerful people on the train. However, she uses her "female empowerment" as an iron fist to ensure no one transgresses their subordinated class position. In another Joon-ho film, *Parasite*, the Kim family rise from being slum-dwelling pizza box assemblers to well-paid domestic workers, living in the wealthy home of their employers. But rather than use their newfound power to build solidarity with other workers, they compete and tear each other down, getting the previous housekeeper fired and leaving her husband in the house's basement to die. In these horror films, the instinct to "lean in" is shown to be a form of brutality that alienates people from each other and from their own humanity.

Read in this light, horror films teach us that we must "lean out" into social solidarity and the struggle for structural change. Whereas mainstream Hollywood genres encourage individualist self-improvement, horror films widen the lens, emphasizing the fact that social injustice cannot be dismantled by a single person. For this reason, the fact that the horror film *The Descent* is populated by "strong female leads" does not lead to the conclusion that these women are "empowered." Instead, it shows a system that offers women only impossible and cruel choices as a female bonding trip turns into an individualistic struggle for bare survival. In order to truly "succeed" we would need an agenda that goes beyond survival to structural change, such as the 2019 wave of women's strikes which, as Cinzia Arruzza argues, have put "women's work, women's role in social reproduction, and the relationship between production of commodities and reproduction at the center of the debate" as well as serving as a means to create "a new anti-capitalist feminist subjectivity."[8] As Patricia Stuelke argues, both women's horror and women's strikes bash back at "the affirmative violence of neoliberal multiculturalism," that is the idea that neoliberalism offers us opportunity simply because there is lip-service to equality.[9] Representing refusal, contemporary horror films can show that class horror is gender horror. And we must think them together.

Social Reproduction Feminism

Social Reproduction feminisms hold that from the beginning, capitalism demanded a separation of spheres. It required "productive" laborers to

---

8 Cinzia Arruzza, "From Women's Strikes to a New Class Movement: The Third Feminist Wave," *Viewpoint Magazine*, December 3, 2018, https://viewpointmag.com/2018/12/03/from-womens-strikes-to-a-new-class-movement-the-third-feminist-wave/.

9 Patricia Stuelke, "Horror and the Arts of Feminist Assembly," *Contemporaries at Post-45*, (April, 2019).

create commodities and to enable capitalism to constantly grow. But it also needed reproductive laborers to ensure that workers were born, raised, fed, and emotionally cared for. Under capitalism, the ongoing strategy to produce and maintain this separation of spheres has always been gendered. As Leopoldina Fortunati pithily puts it, women's reproductive labor is "the creation of value that must appear otherwise."[10] Even though these two forms of labor are equally necessary, by labeling the feminized sphere of labor as less valuable and more natural, the ruling class has successfully blocked solidarity between men and women as well as ensuring free or cheap reproductive labor. At the heart of this division there is ever and always the threat of violence. Domestic violence and state violence follow the same logic. They enforce the rigid gendered division of labor, and demand that the feminine sphere remains lower in the hierarchical order of things, keeping us all running through the endless, byzantine hedge maze of *The Shining* where men, frustrated at their eternal inability to get ahead, project their murderous rage at the wives who make their lives possible.

In her book *Caliban and the Witch*, Silvia Federici traces the origins of this violence to the moment of the transition from feudalism to capitalism. Under the feudal system, women and men often did the same work, and when work was gendered, it was equally valued (or at least more so than at present). Federici argues that in order to force populations to enter into capitalist relations of production, a divide-and-conquer method was employed. By labeling men's productive work as more valuable and offering the possibility of a subordinate female slave as a reward for this labor, capitalists effectively sabotaged solidarity between men and women when both should have been collaborating to defeat the enclosure of their lands and bodies. In order to coerce women into the role of passive, loving helpmeet, the witch hunts were created to punish those who remained ungovernable and unruly.

It took torturing, burning, and drowning so-called witches to turn them into obedient domestic subjects, and yet the work of these subjects is now framed as a "natural" act of love. The 2015 horror film *The Witch* demonstrates this violence as Thomasin, a teenaged girl, is forced into endless

---

10 Leopoldina Fortunati, *The Arcane of Reproduction: Housework, Prostitution, Labor and Capital*, trans. Hillary Creek (Brooklyn: Autonomedia, 1995), 8.

labor for her family and still labeled as a devil-worshipping witch. What is her sin? She unwittingly arouses the incestuous desires of the men around her. In fact, she is put in an impossible situation where she is supposed to both satisfy male desire and avoid the incest taboo. For the inability to solve this impossible contradiction she is punished gravely. However, as in many feminist horror films, *The Witch* shows that the witch hunts could not rid women of their rebellious spirits, and that the identity of "witch" could be appropriated to bash back and "live deliciously."

At the end of *The Witch*, Thomasin leaves her family to live with a coven of witches. We hope her time will be spent flying, dancing naked, and performing strange but consensual rituals with Black Philip, the goat devil who orchestrates her liberation. Before that, however, her life was filled with drudgery as she gathered food, tended animals, and cooked and cleaned for her joyless family. Strangely, in orthodox theories of Marxism this type of labor has often been denied its rightful status as work. As Maya Gonzalez argues, this strict interpretation of Marx leads dogmatic Marxologists to assert that only organizing among laborers traditionally considered to be "productive" can lead to class struggle.[11]

Against this view, Gonzalez argues that feminist theories of reproduction make a *political* point. Women have traditionally inhabited "the hidden abode of labor-power's reproduction," and without the work in this sphere *there could be no wage-relation*. In other words, a productive laborer could never work a forty-hour week for minimum wage without someone in the background preparing "his" food, cleaning "his" clothes, and making "his" life emotionally tolerable. Even if a worker could manage to reproduce themselves alone, they could not provide for future generations of workers.

The invisibility of social reproduction led the important 1970s feminist "Wages for Housework" movement to propose a controversial strategy. After much debate, an international group of feminists decided to launch a campaign to get *paid* for domestic chores. They didn't make this choice because they wanted to be treated *like* male "productive" workers. They wanted to liberate themselves *and* their male comrades

---

11 Maya Gonzalez, "The Gendered Circuit: Reading the Arcane of Reproduction," *Viewpoint*, September 28, 2013, https://viewpointmag.com/2013/09/28/the-gendered-circuit-reading-the-arcane-of-reproduction/.

from exploitative work. But to do this they had to show that their work was essential to the capitalist relation. Housework enabled the wage, it was not simply a moral or emotional issue.

The horror outlined by social reproduction theories, then, is a kind of gaslighting of people who perform work outside the officially designated "point of production," such as the factory or other obvious places of commodity production. In their exclusion from definitions of value and from categories of work that could build solidarity and class struggle, women and other feminized people are rendered mute and helpless. They are, as Selma James insists, "a hidden reserve work force," where "unemployed women work behind closed doors at home, to be called out again when capital needs them elsewhere."[12] In having their work deemed as natural, women are alienated from their own suffering and desire to revolt. The silent scream a woman might nurse in the back of her throat as she cooks, cleans, and tends the baby can never escape her, lest she be accused of failing to love her family or of failing to behave as a "real woman."

However, in horror she screams and screams loudly. Just look at Ari Aster's 2018 film *Hereditary,* where the protagonist Annie experiences her family as an endless psychological assault and lets everyone in earshot know by wielding her voice as one long wail of sorrow. It seems that a mother could never grieve too much for a dead daughter, but in this film, her child's death seems to liberate Annie from the family altogether, as she renounces all motherly duties and enters a world of pure, horrific emotion. In Aster's next film, *Midsommar,* a similar effect is deployed as protagonist Dani's sobs are unnaturally amplified to stress the horror of familial trauma. Both of these films "seem to open otherworldly portals to their own powers of horror," Sophie Lewis argues, by operatically staging the deeply intimate horror of the family. Lewis concludes, "To abolish the family, these images seem to whisper, would be to abolish the self..."[13]

---

12 Mariarosa Dalla Costa and Selma James, *Women and the Subversion of Community* (Bristol: Falling Wall Press, 1972), 10.

13 Sophie Lewis, "The Satanic Death Cult is Real," *Commune,* Aug. 28, 2019, https://communemag.com/the-satanic-death-cult-is-real/.

Neoliberal Necropolitics

We tend to think of the gendered division of labor by imagining the middle-class housewife in her private sphere. And of course, this was one way that capitalism attained free labor. With the "family wage," only one member of a family needed to be paid, while the housewife would tend to "his" needs outside of work. At the same time she would produce and raise future laborers. However, this model of analysis has always been complicated by the fact that poor women and women of color typically worked both inside and outside of the home, saddled with what Angela Davis and others call a "double burden."[14]

Even when the housewife held a significant social position, she was not the only role enforced by the gendered division of labor, nor the most oppressed example. Now, in a moment in which more women are entering the workforce, we are grappling even more with the adaptability of the gendered division of labor. "Capitalism has been spectacularly successful in using the gender distinction toward its own ends," as Juliana Spahr and Joshua Clover argue, and this mutability has allowed the role of housewife to define wildly diverse forms of reproductive labor and activity.[15] Even in 1975, Mariarosa Dalla Costa and Selma James, proponents of the "Wages for Housework" movement, declared: "We assume that all women are housewives and even those who work outside the home continue to be housewives."[16]

Capitalism adapted to women entering the workforce in a moment when service labor, flexible labor, and affective labor were simultaneously expanding. As these forms of labor grew, they were also degraded as "feminine" endeavors. The position of today's "precariat"—workers whose labor is part-time, low-waged, and insecure—consists of many feminized roles such as gig workers, service

14 Angela Davis, "The Approaching Obsolescence of Housework," *Revolutionary Feminism: Communist Intervention Series*, 3, 363.

15 Joshua Clover and Juliana Spahr, "Gender Abolition and Ecotone War," *South Atlantic Quarterly*, 115, no. 2, (2016): 297.

16 Mariarosa Dalla Costa and Selma James, *The Power of Women and the Subversion of the Community*, 2.

workers, health workers, sex workers, nannies, and housekeepers. The common thread is low wages, few protections, and lack of worker's control.

This manipulation of "cheap short-term flexible labor-power under globalized conditions of accumulation" is how the Endnotes collective define contemporary "feminization."[17] To explain the turn to neoliberalism and the consequent feminization of labor we can briefly sketch the large economic and social transformations that led to a shift in the current logic of capital and the expansion of "feminized" labor. While this is not the place to get into a detailed description of all the factors that went into constructing our moment of neoliberal precarity and austerity, it helps to have a few markers to guide our understanding of the contemporary capitalist dynamics leading up to this "feminization."

First, we should understand this as a shift away from Fordism—a system in place in roughly the first half of the 20th century marked by mass production, unionization, and Keynesianism (significant social entitlements such as welfare, public education, and social security). Marxist geographer David Harvey and others theorize this transition as a response to capitalist crisis tendencies. Built into capitalism is both a need for constant accumulation of profit as well as contradictions that eventually lead to crises of this accumulation. Some of the factors that led to the implosion of Fordism were overproduction of commodities and consequent declines in corporate productivity and profitability.[18] At the same time, the increase in production in less developed nations led multinational corporations to invest in offshore manufacturing, where they could avoid Fordist unions and labor laws, instead offering workers low wages and insecurity, and by doing so, strengthening their own profits.[19] Additionally, it became clear that the Fordist system was too rigid and inflexible to cope with the increasing global complexity of the market. The strength of unions under Fordism ensured that when corporations tried to dismantle the "rigid" securities of

---

17 Endnotes collective, "The Logic of Gender," *Endnotes* 3, https://endnotes.org.uk/issues/3/en/endnotes-the-logic-of-gender.
18 David Harvey, *The Condition of Postmodernity* (Blackwell, 1991), 141.
19 Harvey, *Condition*, 141.

the system, workers could fight back.[20] And the commitment of the Fordist state to provide basic social protections also hindered "flexibility."[21] A sharp recession in the 1970s delivered a final blow to the "Fordist compromise" and set in full motion a regime marked by deindustrialization, the breaking up of unions, the expansion of free market policies, privatization, deregulation, financialization, and the dismantling of social protections.

Harvey frames this turn from Fordism to post-Fordism as "flexible accumulation"—a period marked by flexibility in all areas, as in "labour processes, labour markets, products, and patterns of consumption."[22] In the US it was marked by a shift to a FIRE economy (Finance, Insurance, Real Estate), and a boom in technology, communication, and the service industry. As Sianne Ngai and many others argue, the rise of these jobs forced workers to "put to work. . . competences once viewed as outside capital," such as "affect, subjectivity, and sociability."[23] This means that forms of feminized labor and social performance considered to be natural and distant from capitalism's process of extracting surplus labor were recognized and further entrenched as central to capitalist accumulation.

Nancy Fraser frames this as the shift from "state-managed capitalism" that promoted the "family wage" and the relegation of women to the home to "globalizing financialized capitalism," in which women were increasingly conscripted to wage labor while programs of social of welfare were strategically neglected, "externalizing carework onto families and communities while diminishing their capacity to perform it." The rise of debt as a driver of the economy was to "intensify capitalism's inherent contradiction between economic production and social reproduction." The effect of impoverishing households while touting diversity resulted in a two-tiered system where working women filled the "care gap" in their households with racialized, "imported" workers, who must abandon their own families, thereby displacing the care gap to poor and rural areas.[24]

20 Harvey, *Condition*, 142.

21 This is not to romanticize Fordism, which truly was a compromise that benefited capitalism and wielded both carrots and sticks to enforce gendered and racial hierarchies while quashing revolutionary forms of solidarity.

22 Harvey, *Condition*, 147.

23 Sianne Ngai, *Our Aesthetic Categories* (Cambridge, MA: Harvard University Press, 2012), 202.

24 Fraser, "Contradictions of Capital and Care."

Stepford Daughters

With these transformations came a rise in unemployment and a "radical restructuring" of the labor market, which enabled a dismantling of Fordist securities, living wages, and public assistance programs such as food stamps and welfare—the means of social reproduction.[25] Like all forms of production, jobs became "flexible," with a rise of part time work, temporary work, gig work, and work without benefits. That is, there is a ratcheting up of *vulnerability* for workers as the meager protections once offered are stripped away. At the same time, "the state launched a violent offensive to irreversibly disrupt the political bases of working-class social reproduction," with the rhetoric of law and order used to deprive people of color and the poor of basic rights and freedoms.[26]

I remember witnessing this transition up close, as my family underwent a common metamorphosis between the late seventies and early eighties. As in a horror movie, one night I went to bed, thinking bright thoughts about my well-employed father, my housewife mother, and my cozily decorated home. In the morning I woke up in a seedy apartment listening to my divorced parents arguing about money on the phone, hoping that my dad would land a job before the first of the month and that my mom's new underpaid job as a microwave salesperson didn't mean that I had to eat a microwaved dinner every night. It goes without saying that I thought we were the only family who were suffering this way. Little did I know that securities and protections were being systematically dismantled for the majority of us. In this programmatic immiseration, our rulers used the language of horror. As Ronald Reagan's ghoulish head pronounced on the TV, "the nine most terrifying words in the English language are 'I'm from the government and I'm here to help.'" By demonizing the basic protections the government offered, along with "welfare mothers," "crackheads," "super predators," and other specters of poverty, the Reagan administration effectively condoned the slow or fast death of those of us who couldn't make it in the libertarian, yuppified, cannibalistic hellscape of the eighties.

In her book, *Work Won't Love You Back*, Sarah Jaffe periodizes neoliberalism by focusing on two of its monsters—Chilean dictator Augusto Pinochet and British Prime Minister Margaret Thatcher. Pinochet coupled

25 Harvey, *Condition*, 150.
26 Mohandesi and Teitelman, "No Reserves," 63.

the ushering-in of a neoliberal economy with the murder of his socialist predecessor, Salvador Allende, and the killing, disappearing, and torture of his country's political dissidents. Margaret Thatcher unleashed a regime of privatization and austerity, justifying this by offering the slogan of TINA (There Is No Alternative). Thatcher's programs ravaged sites of community, instead offering only "the pleasures of cruelty, the negative solidarity, that is, of seeing others even worse off than themselves by cuts in the welfare state."[27] For Jaffe, these true monsters of neoliberalism are symbolic of the ways that late capitalist logic robbed people of their most precious resource, the ability to experience solidarity and love outside the workplace.

As a consequence of this denial of love and social solidarity, Jaffe argues, people began to love their work rather than each other. Having formed this abusive attachment with their jobs and denied the Fordist protections of unions, people had no way to fight back against austerity and precarity. The only possible way to respond to a job that "fail[s] to love you back" is "to work harder on yourself or leave."[28]

This universal call for self-reliance without offering people collective solutions exposes the neoliberal turn as a failure. Rather than solving the contradictions of Fordism, our moment has revealed the system to be in permanent crisis. In true horror mode, Joshua Clover compares this undead system to a zombie, "shambling forward, hungry and blindly grasping."[29] And this zombie capitalism leads to zombified subjects. The permanent crisis of capital ends in what the philosopher Achille Mbembe calls "necro-politics," a system that not only actively kills people, but also has the power to expel people, to cast them into social and political death, or to simply let them physically die through neglect.

The Powers of Horror

In 1978 the Marxist, queer film critic Robin Wood made the convincing case that there is no better film genre than horror to express and contest

---

27 Sarah Jaffe, *Work Won't Love You Back: How Devotion to Our Jobs Keeps Us Exploited, Exhausted, and Alone* (New York: Bold Type Books, 2021), 7.

28 Jaffe, *Work Won't Love You Back*, 9.

29 Joshua Clover, "Swans and Zombies: Neoliberalism's Permanent Contradiction, " *The Nation*, Apr. 25, 2011, https://www.thenation.com/article/ swans-and-zombies-neoliberalisms-permanent-contradiction/.

the oppressions of capitalist patriarchy. Our culture, he argued, operates by forcing us to repress every thought, impulse, and emotion that goes against a standard of normalcy dictated by bourgeois patriarchy. He starts by looking at the ways our wild and abundant sexual energies are tamed in modern US culture, where we are compelled to channel all of our eros into heterosexual monogamy and boring jobs. Desires that would inspire us to experiment with alternate forms of sexuality and creativity are seen as transgressive and taboo. Any violation of strict gender and sexuality categories is seen as a threat to the reproductive family. Capitalism depends on upholding strict masculine and feminine roles, and will not stand to be challenged. Women's aggression or desire, too, must be repressed; her subordinate role must be naturalized and affirmed.

Wood claims that this repression creates the category of "the other," "that which bourgeois ideology cannot recognize or accept."[30] These repressed "others" appear in horror films as monstrous sources of fear. Says Wood, "the true subject of the horror genre is the struggle for recognition of all that our civilization represses or oppresses." The reemergence of these repressions is dramatized as a horror, as in our nightmares.[31]

Horror films grapple directly with repressed forms of sexuality and violence through fantasy and the supernatural. As Wood argues, this connects the genre with dreams and nightmares, the theater where repressed desires may surface in disguised forms. Horror films, as opposed to "social issue" films, are escapist. But it is that very escapism that allows unconscious elements to make themselves known. As "collective nightmares," horror films work their way around ideological censorship, by appearing as merely frivolous and trashy entertainment.[32]

Relating to Wood's criticism, Barbara Creed and other psychoanalytically oriented feminist critics point to horror film as a privileged genre to explore the repressed, which they call "abjection." In the psychoanalytic model the *abject* is a product of a child's development. The child is born into a "semiotic" stage where she is at one with the mother and is not yet entered

---

30 Robin Wood, "An Introduction to the American Horror Film," in *On the Horror Film: Collected Essays and Reviews*, edited by Barry Keith Grant (Detroit: Wayne State University Press 2018), 77.

31 Wood, "An Introduction," 79.

32 Wood, "An Introduction," 83.

into language and the "symbolic order." But in the next stage, the child must separate herself from the mother and live within the strictures of "the law of the Father," where patriarchal rules govern the social. This separation from the mother, however, is always haunted by the past. The maternal threatens to bleed past the psychic boundaries that contain and repress her. Thus, rationality is threatened by the *abject* mother, whose qualities and substances inspire revulsion and terror. For Creed and others, horror movies represent elements that the dominant patriarchal culture qualifies as "feminine" and deems unspeakably grotesque, such as irrationality, emotionality, and indeterminacy as well as bodily excesses related to menstruation, sexuality, and pregnancy.

In horror films like *Possession* and *The Untamed* this repressed abjection reemerges in the form of Lovecraftian monstrosity in women who find themselves enveloped and penetrated by slimy tentacular monsters, while in French extreme horror like *Raw, Trouble Everyday,* and *In My Skin* cannibalism and self-mutilation evoke this disgust and fascination with female bodies and sexuality. Many of these films build on the "body horror" pioneered by David Cronenberg in the 1980s where, as Steven Shaviro argues, characters die through feminized excess, "each in his or her own way is made pregnant with a monstrous birth."[33] These horrors especially occur in the claustrophobic interiors structured by the family, or what Tony Williams, in his examination of the genre's macabre view of the nuclear family, calls "Hearths of Darkness."

This repression is not only psychic but social and historical, which contributes to the gothic aesthetic of many horror films. As Teresa Goddu argues, national history and self-mythologization is created through displacement and exclusion. Gothic themes have always served as a kind of resurrection of the repressed, "disrupt[ing] the dream world of national myth with the nightmares of history." [34] Sheri-Marie Harrison argues that the gothic "tropes of darkness, madness, ghosts, and isolation" bring

33 Steven Shaviro, *Cinematic Body* (Minneapolis: University of Minnesota Press, 1989), 131.
34 Teresa Goddu, *Gothic America: Narrative, History, and Nation* (New York: Columbia University Press, 1997), 10.

historical repression of slavery, exploitation, genocide to the surface.[35] The female gothic represents not only the horrors of history but the fact that women have been erased from history. Historically speaking, women are always ghosts and specters, as our confinement to the private sphere has equated to a kind of public death. Even after women have emerged into public life, we are associated with the private, with passivity, and lack, and these associations have deprived us of substantive representation. Horror films like *The Others*, in which a woman goes through life not knowing she is a ghost, force us to confront these historical erasures.

Horror films' monsters and menaces are often described as uncanny. As Freud famously argued, the uncanny is a feeling of terror or alienation in the face of a phenomena that is familiar. The German word for uncanny is *unheimlich*, a word that can mean both "familiar and agreeable" and "concealed and kept out of sight."[36] The word also refers to the home, conjuring the domestic horrors women face. The feeling of uncanniness arises not despite familiarity, but because of familiarity, showing that the source of horror is not strangers or alien forces, but our most intimate relations and conditions.

The horror genre is littered with life-like dolls, mysterious doppelgangers, bodies possessed by demons and monsters, and bodies that are neither alive nor dead. These phenomena haunt us because of their proximity to ourselves, not because they are simply alien or different. True terror always lies menacingly close, in the sphere of intimacy. In that sense we can interpret the underworld doppelgangers in the horror film *Us* as a form of what Marina Vishmidt calls "reproductive realism."[37] Here, the monsters are us, shown as bare forms of life, stripped of all illusions of freedom. They capture the ways that capitalism turns us into puppets, whose strings are pulled by unknown forces as we reproduce our daily lives.

Introduction

---

35   Sheri-Marie Harrison, "New Black Gothic," *Los Angeles Review of Books*, June 23, 2018, https://lareviewofbooks.org/article/new-black-gothic/.

36   Sigmund Freud, "The Uncanny," in *The Standard Edition of the Complete Psychological Works of Sigmund Freud*, trans. James Strachey (London: The Hogarth Press, 1917–1919), 225.

37   Marina Vishmidt, "Reproductive Realism: Towards a Critical Aesthetics of Gendered Labor," *Histórias Feministas seminar* (Museu de Arte São Paulo, 2018).

In response to this enforced passivity, horror's "final girls," the survivor figures who Carol Clover argues becomes the source of the horror viewer's identification, have become more complicated.[38] Rather than as innocent victims, women are seen as figures of retributive violence that is not always able to be rationalized as fair or heroic. As Neal King and Martha McCaughey argue, violent women in film are always shocking. Even feminist critics will insist that positive women characters should embrace the "feminine" quality of non-violence.[39] However, in horror women have access to what Jack Halberstam, following June Jordan, calls "a place of rage," referring to rage that is justified and necessary for self-defense. The representation of women committing acts of violence in horror allows for an opening, he says, "between and beyond thought, action, response, activism, protest, anger, terror, murder, and detestation."[40] Retributive violence shifts the ground of agency, showing that capitalist violence may not be able to continue with impunity.

In the films explored in this book, we will see "violent" women and girls. Revenge here, however, is not a tool of suppression, but a way to break psychological and material chains that will otherwise, as Franz Fanon insists, forever bind "the wretched of the earth." These films are negative but not nihilistic. We can think of the forms of refusal we see in horror next to the anti-work theories of autonomist Marxists who felt that refusal was not simply abdicating work, but rather pointing to rich forms of political community and a reorganization of society that lay beyond the logic of work. Work refusal, Kathi Weeks suggests, should "be understood as a creative practice, one that seeks to reappropriate and reconfigure existing forms of production and reproduction."[41] In this way, the negation found in horror films can be seen as a creative, hopeful act.

---

38 Carol J. Clover, *Men Women, and Chain Saws: Gender in the Modern Horror Film* (Princeton: Princeton University Press, 2003).

39 Neal King and Martha McCaughey, "What's a Mean Woman like You Doing in a Movie Like This," in *Reel Knockouts: Violent Women in Film*, edited by Neal King and Martha McCaughey (Austin: University of Texas Press, 2001).

40 Jack Halberstam, "Imagined Violence/Queer Violence: Representations of Rage and Resistance," in *Reel Knockouts: Violent Women in Film*, edited by Neal King and Martha McCaughey (Austin: University of Texas Press, 2001), 247.

41 Kathi Weeks, *The Problem with Work* (Durham: Duke University Press, 2011), 99.

From Hearths of Darkness to Coming-of-Rage

Whereas horror has always provided a way to explore repressed anger and desire, the present is a unique moment. In the past, directors and writers of horror have been overwhelmingly male. This is changing. In this book I look closely at twenty films. I did not pay attention to the gender of directors or writers when selecting these films. They were picked because they addressed the themes I felt were most relevant to the questions I wanted to ask about gendered capitalism. Still, seven out of the twenty directors are women. Only four of the films were directed by white men. This reflects a sea change in the visions expressed in horror that is providing a richer set of voices and visions.

This contrasts current trends in Hollywood film, where women and people of color are still lacking representation. The industry tends to "follow the money," as Jon Lewis argues.[42] Since the era of the blockbuster and greater conglomeration, the industry has assigned more and more importance to box office sales. This, in combination with white male domination at every level of Hollywood production, ensures that the stories and voices of marginalized people are rarely told. Statistics are disheartening. In the first decade of the twenty-first century, Black filmmakers only directed seven percent of Hollywood films. Seventy-five percent of actors who appear in film and TV are white, with Latinos being the most underrepresented race. Although Latinos comprise sixteen percent of the population, they play five percent of speaking characters.[43] Eighty percent of feature film writers are white.[44] While women are more represented as actors, they only work about seventeen percent of the behind-the-scenes roles on high-grossing films. Women have never reached over ten percent of directors of feature films, and in most genres this number shows trends of declining.[45]

42 Jon Lewis, "Following the Money in America's Sunniest Company Town: Some Notes on the Political Economy of the Hollywood Blockbuster," in *Movie Blockbusters*, edited by Julian Stringer, (London: Routledge, 2003), 63.

43 Maryann Erigha, "Race, Gender, Hollywood: Representation in Cultural Production and Digital Media's Potential for Change," *Sociology Compass* 9, no. 1, (January 2015), 82.

44 Erigha, "Race, Gender, Hollywood," 82.

45 Erigha, "Race, Gender, Hollywood," 83.

Horror, however, shows more promise, with higher percentages of woman directors and behind-the-scenes workers.[46] This is partially because horror can be made for less money, and now can be distributed in new ways, such as through internet and streaming services.[47] As Evelyn Wang argues, we have recently seen a new wave of "horror classics about women, by women." With a rising number of woman journalists and a blurring between "arthouse" movies and horror, there are more opportunities for women to make their voices heard.[48]

While the participation of women in key roles of film production is essential to making the horror genre more relevant to feminists, this book is not interested in fetishizing the identity of film creators or characters. Rather, I am trying to read films as tools for feminists to understand key problems that face us in the real world and also to insist that we all have the capability to *interpret* cultural works we love to support our own struggles. While I do have an academic degree, I am not trained in film studies. My film criticism and this book have been a labor of love done outside the academy or any paid journalism. I began publishing essays on films in the radical cultural journal *Blind Field*, an all-volunteer publication, and other leftist venues, because of my love for horror and my desire to read about film from a radical, feminist perspective. I was writing the articles that I wanted to read but couldn't find in the mainstream press, where these themes are heavily censored or simply not part of the cultural "common sense." I found that even when reviewers do attempt to address complex political themes in popular culture, the space allotted to them in newspapers and magazines is not adequate to go very deep. More than that, our culture creates a radical divide between popular criticism and academic criticism that limits the tools available to feminists and radicals who are outside the academy.

Personally, I think that we are in a stage of history where we desperately need what Raymond Williams called an emergent "structure of feeling" that is leftist and feminist. As we are inundated with the language of

---

46 Erigha, "Race, Gender, Hollywood," 85.

47 Erigha, "Race, Gender, Hollywood," 88.

48 Evelyn Wang, "Welcome to the Golden Age of Woman-Directed Horror," *Vice*, April 14, 2017, https://www.vice.com/en/article/zmbnd5/ welcome-to-the-golden-age-of-women-directed-horror.

austerity, capitalist realism, and moderation, cultural criticism can be a site for what second-wave feminists called consciousness raising. We need a common language to explain the transformations of the work world and everyday life and to articulate our own opposition and hopes for a radically transformed horizon. When I was younger, I used to attend anarchist "skill shares," workshops where people contributed whatever they could to the general knowledge. In that spirit, I see this book as a place to share tools and weapons to reclaim the culture we love for the world we want to see.

The chapters in this book will cover what I see as the most mystified areas of social life in our moment. Most of the films were made after the 2008 real-estate market crash and reflect the intensified contradictions that beset us after this financial crisis. The first chapter is about the home and family as horror, but also how this family form spills out into waged work. In *Hereditary*, *The Babadook*, *Under the Shadow*, *Dark Water*, and *The Happiness of the Katakuris*, home is where the hellfire is. But the monstrosity of enforced familial roles does not end at the front door. In Chapter Two I turn to the films *Housekeeping*, *The Maid*, *Get Out*, *La Llorona*, and *Good Manners* to examine racialized waged reproductive labor in horror. The commonplace face of domestic work is the white middle-class housewife, but the reality is that the bulk of reproductive laborers are rendered invisible and hyper-exploited, saddled with the "double burden" of low waged and unwaged domestic work. The films in this chapter render the violence of hyper-exploitation visible. Chapter Three looks at how the films *Maps to the Stars*, *Parasite*, *I Blame Society*, *Cam*, and *Sorry to Bother You* navigate contemporary forms of emotional labor. What kind of horrors follow when workers are estranged from their own smiles? How do we understand our own feelings when love becomes our job? The loveless and unloved figures of horror help us map the cracks in the seemingly smooth surfaces of emotional labor. Chapter Four examines girls' coming-of-age stories in horror films such as *It Follows*, *Assassination Nation*, *The Fits*, *The Lure*, and *Teeth*. I ask, what does it mean for "generation rent" to come of age into the "bullshit jobs," precarious jobs, or joblessness of late capitalist futurelessness? And how do young women resist the imperative to assimilate as self-entrepreneurs and instead mature into warriors? Finally, the conclusion will be a personal meditation on the strange hopefulness that "becoming monster" can offer feminists.

I hope that by the end of this book the reader will see that contemporary horror films do not only diagnose the crisis of care and the feminization of labor that characterize our moment, but also create memorable figures of refusal and resistance. Even though horror is seen by some as a genre that promotes nihilism, I will make the case that these films can provide feminist radicals with weapons to confront complacency and hopelessness.

CHAPTER ONE

IT'S COMING FROM INSIDE/OUTSIDE THE HOUSE: HORROR AS CARE STRIKE

In the film *When a Stranger Calls*, a young babysitter sits in a suburban home. The phone rings. A creepy voice asks her, "have you checked the children?" Panicked, she searches the empty, darkened rooms. What should seem comfortable and familiar is suddenly uncanny. The neat kitchen counter menaces. The ice cubes that rattle in the freezer startle. The phone rings again. The stranger is out there, watching her. She can feel his gaze. She tries to convince the dismissive police to help. Begrudgingly, they finally agree to put a trace on the call. The phone rings again. She keeps him on the line. "What do you want?" she asks. "Your blood. All over me," he responds. The police phone again. They have traced the call. It's coming from inside the house.

The Home as Horror

For women, the home is not a safe place. Feminists know that the terror is not just out there, distant from our secure homes. We know that domestic chores and domestic violence threaten us at every turn. The statistics are a horror show themselves. Every year, more than ten million people are physically abused by an intimate partner. One in ten women have been raped by a partner. Seventy-two percent of all murder-suicides involve an intimate partner. One in fifteen children is exposed to intimate partner violence every year.[1] Statistics about domestic violence are not complete

---

1 "Statistics," *NCADV* (National Coalition Against Domestic Violence, 2021), https://ncadv. org/STATISTICS.

for the period of the COVID-19 pandemic but all available information points to a sharp spike even above these terrifying numbers. Around the world, abuse rose up to 300 percent. In the US, cities reported huge jumps in domestic violence reports and hospitals have witnessed spikes in injuries consistent with abuse.[2]

At the same time that we can take note of these statistics, the terrors coming from inside the house occur even when there is no physical violence. Having one's work and needs denigrated and ignored is itself a form of violence. As Silvia Federici and Nicole Cox argued in their influential tract "Counterplanning from the Kitchen," the tendency to naturalize and dismiss domestic work is overwhelming in our society. Women's domestic labor is seen as private and lesser than the "productive" public work done in the factory. A housewife may work to care for her family from dusk until dawn, and yet, unlike her waged husband, in the eyes of the world she does not "work." The danger of this ideology is that it is used to keep women indentured to the home and family, and to mystify even the most exhausting work as pure love.

In mainstream popular culture, the domestic house is imagined as a place of fullness, warmth, and tenderness. But horror exposes its dark underbelly. In season two of the horror TV show *Channel Zero: No-End House*, Margot, an unhappy young woman who has recently lost her father, is swallowed up by a haunted house attraction. There, she comes to live in a stark suburb where she is showered with love by her now-alive father and new boyfriend Seth. Seth is seductive, "I know you. I see the real you," he says. "As long as you are here, I will always, always be there for you." She becomes so attached that she starts to forget who she is. Only when it is nearly too late does she see the house for what it is, a vampire disguised as shelter. In a cul-de-sac Seth keeps the women he had loved before her in identical suburban homes. We learn that the house eats the memories and minds of these women until they finally shamble around as drained zombie husks, with only one word left in their vocabulary—Seth.

Here, horror turns the naturalized sphere of domestic life inside-out. Instead of a peaceful refuge from cruel public life, home is where the hellfire

---

2 Jeffrey Kluger, "Domestic Violence is a Pandemic Within the COVID 19 Pandemic," *Time*, February 3, 2021, https://time.com/5928539/domestic-violence-covid-19/.

is. Fantasized as the homely source of love and light, in real life, the family sphere is often a "hearth of darkness," as Tony Williams argues.[3] Home is where individuals, born with infinite potential, are wrenched into a form that is pleasing and useful to patriarchal capitalism, deprived of autonomy and genuine choice. In the traditional nuclear family, fathers feel compelled to adapt authoritarian stances and to define themselves by their wage-earning potential. Mothers are prohibited from expressing their own desires, and instead must dedicate themselves to selfless care. Children are pressured to reproduce the heteronormative rituals of their parents and to repress impulses to find their own forms of self-expression and sexuality. This is dramatized in horror, as flesh-and-blood women become Stepford automatons, living to find the perfect brand of cleanser. As in the films *The Texas Chainsaw Massacre*, *We Are What We Are*, and *Raw*, the family becomes a cannibalistic nightmare doomed to repeat. Starving for emotional and material resources made scarce by neoliberal austerity, the family devours itself.

Says Tony Williams, "[The family] has a specific social and psychic function, policing desire, social relations, and artistic expression."[4] Much of feminist horror criticism has explored this process through Freudian language. Freud's well-known description of gendered socialization is the Oedipus complex, in which male children are forced to reject the mother and look toward the father as a model for identification. It is only this repression that gives men access to patriarchal power. On the other hand, female children must accept their subordinate difference and their lack of the phallus. This process is aided by the "good mother" who devotes herself to selfless nurturing in the name of her child's development. The child embraces "the law of the father," which is the same as the law of society, and she renounces "the potentially dangerous, engulfing maternal body."[5]

If one fails this process of Oedipalization, bad things happen, as we see in David Cronenberg's most questionable film, *The Brood*, in which a woman gives birth to children who are simply her own psychic projections,

3 Tony Williams, *Hearths of Darkness: The Family in American Horror Film* (Jackson: University Press of Mississippi, 2015), 15.
4 Williams, *Hearths of Darkness*, 15.
5 Erin Harrington, *Women, Monstrosity and Horror Film: Gynaehorror* (London: Routledge, 2017), 186.

and who exist only to act out her unconscious, destructive desires. If, on the other hand, a person navigates the Oedipal process successfully and mother and child separate in the prescribed way, this becomes a ticket to normality; the lucky winner can begin a family of her own! But what about those of us who fail or opt out? Horror, a world that defies conventions, gives us a glimpse of outliers: fantastic beings and monsters who have refused to be good boys and girls.

Abolish the Family!

Horror films disturb us when they don't attempt to cure or reunite families but instead trigger the family's destruction, as in the world-demolishing ending of *Hereditary*, in which a disintegrating finally implodes, with all members ending up possessed, beheaded, or burnt to a crisp. This refusal corresponds with a strategy Marxist-feminists have come up with to respond to the instrumentalization of the family—"family abolition." Kathi Weeks explains that the term, which is so controversial now, was a common feminist goal in the 1970s. Marxist-feminists of that time made the case that in order to fight capitalism, it was important to "examine how labor power was reproduced on a daily basis." "The family," Weeks argues, "is the way most of us are recruited into households, and how our roles and obligations to the household are determined."[6] In other words, a core way we form our identity is not simply as a person, nor even a man or woman, but as a mother, father, son, daughter, or some combination of these positions.

In response to a tidal wave of negative reaction to and misunderstanding of the call for "family abolition," feminists backed off from that goal and instead fought for more inclusive families. But Weeks insists that we must return to abolition in order to understand the family as an institution that perpetuates capitalist domination. She builds on Angela Davis' structural analysis of the prison system by "going after the family, not particular families." So, even though many families are loving and supportive, the family structure itself is killing us.

6   Kathi Weeks, "Abolish the Family!" *Red May*, May 29, 2020, https://www.youtube.com/watch?v=8nfeTeUgBZg.

This is not because people in families don't love each other. Rather, it is because the family becomes an excuse to privatize the process of reproduction (feeding, clothing, housing, caring for people) instead of offering external support. Faced with a social void, the family has to take on all this work itself. Whereas the family and all social forms should be solely dedicated to love, care, mutual aid, and creativity, the family is instead wrenched into the service of capitalism, taking care of the duties that would be more humanely provided by the public.

For many families, this is an unbearable pressure. Not only is it impossible for most families to serve as an oasis in the middle of an austere desert, the reliance on the family serves as a rationalization for leaving people who are separated or estranged from their families completely abandoned. As Michelle O'Brien notes, the family "bundles both necessary forms of care and isolation."[7] That is, the family creates the condition where a person can't be guaranteed care without submitting themselves to whatever the family wants of them. Thus if they are from an abusive, homophobic, or otherwise dysfunctional family they have no way out. And if the family unit can't earn enough money to reproduce itself, they are left with no option but disintegration. Sometimes this disintegration is forced, as we've seen in recent family separations at the border. As Melinda Cooper notes in her important book, *Family Values*, arch-capitalist Thomas Friedman himself points out that "this is really a family society, not an individual society." The greatest incentive to self-sacrifice and personal immiseration is the fantasy of the family.[8] Because of these constraints, our deification of the conventional family unit kind of makes sense, but existing families can't bear it.

The family is both "a welcome sanctuary and a trap," as Weeks puts it. For some, the family is a source of love and protection in a cruelly atomizing world. But many must strike a devil's bargain, submitting themselves to cruelty and coercion in order to get the succor they need. As Walter Benjamin put it, "how radical [capitalism] is can be seen in its attitude toward the

---

7 Michelle O'Brien, "Abolish the Family!" *Red May*, May 29, 2020, https://www.youtube.com/watch?v=8nfeTeUgBZg.

8 Melinda Cooper, Family *Values: Between Neoliberalism and the New Social Conservatism* (Brooklyn: Zone Books, 2017), 59.

family.... It insists upon the family at any price, even where intensification of family life can only aggravate the suffering already caused by conditions utterly unworthy of human beings."[9]

Hereditary: The Family as Horrible Helpless Machine

In the 2018 horror film *Hereditary* family life is nothing if not intense. In the central family's household, the great miseries that have haunted bourgeois domesticity for centuries seem to all be crammed together in a claustrophobic hot house of explosive emotions. Annie, the mother and protagonist, both lives in and recreates this condensed space in the form of haunted dollhouses. Her creations show that the same wraiths that stalk the "hearths of darkness" in the domestic home now lurk in so-called "public spaces," where feminized care work is performed.

Since the emergence of Henrik Ibsen's groundbreaking 1879 feminist play *A Doll's House*, the miniature home has been a symbol of women's domestic entrapment. Doll houses, Gwynne Watkins argues, are "handy miniature metaphors" that represent domestic interiors of fear.[10] Similarly, Anna Leszkiewicz explains that the dollhouses that populate recent films and TV shows serve to "unlock ... the secrets of the real home."[11] In *Hereditary*, the dollhouses Annie makes echo the prison-like coldness and claustrophobia of her family home.

* * *

Before I proceed, I want to note that *Hereditary*, like all the films discussed in this book, will be completely "spoiled." I recommended watching them

---

9 Walter Benjamin, "A Family Drama in the Epic Theater," *Walter Benjamin: Selected Writings, Volume 2: Part 2: 1927–1930*, ed. Michael W. Jennings, Howard Eiland, and Gary Smith (Cambridge: Belknap Press 2005), 559.

10 Gwynne Watkins, "A Guide to the Most Delightful—And Sinister—Dollhouses in Pop Culture," *Vulture*, July 19, 2018, https://www.vulture.com/2018/07/a-guide-to-delightful-and-sinister-pop-culture-dollhouses.html.

11 Anna Leszkiewicz, "The Rise of the Creepy Doll's House," *New Statesman*, October 31, 2018, https://www.newstatesman.com/culture/film/2018/10/dolls-houses-hereditary-sharp-objects-miniaturist-halloween-dollhouse.

before you read if you're not a weirdo like me who actually seeks out spoilers!

Hereditary begins with the funeral of Annie's mother, Ellen, a woman the protagonist evidently has ambivalent feelings towards, as we see from her eulogy that includes very little praise and many allusions to her mother's secrecy and opaqueness. After the funeral, the family seems mostly unaffected, but Annie's thirteen-year-old daughter, Charlie, is truly disturbed by the loss of her grandmother. Charlie is an uncanny, asocial child who dresses in gender non-conforming baggy clothing and is obsessed with drawing cryptic pictures of birds, constructing totemic toys, and methodically eating chocolate. She often disturbs her family by making haunting clicking sounds and sleeping in a cold treehouse outside the home rather than in her bedroom.

Following her grandmother's death, Charlie's behavior becomes increasingly odd. A bird crashes into her schoolroom window and she secretly clips off its head, saving it for a private ritual she will perform in her backyard. Trying to help her child integrate socially, Annie forces her teenaged son, Peter, to take Charlie to a party, where he suggests she eat some chocolate cake while he smokes pot with a girl who interests him. The cake activates Charlie's nut allergy and her throat closes up. Peter rushes to drive her to the hospital when an animal jumps in front of the car just as she is sticking her head out the window, gasping for breath. Peter swerves and hits a telephone pole, beheading his sister.

When Annie finds Charlie dead, her desolation is operatic. She wails and screams from the moment she finds the body until it is lowered into the ground. This is not only a mother's grief. We have learned that Annie's family history is terrifying. Her mother was plagued with dissociative identity disorder, and her consequent erratic behavior contributed to the family's total decimation. Annie's father killed himself by starvation and her brother hanged himself, blaming his mother for "putting people inside him." It seems that only Annie and her children are left to carry on the family's genes and dysfunction.

When Annie seeks help from a support group, she is intercepted by Joan, a figure who while seemingly maternal and sympathetic, clearly has

35

an agenda—pushing Annie to explore psychic phenomena that will help her communicate with her dead daughter. Eventually Joan persuades Annie to perform a mysterious ritual in her home that includes her entire family, summoning Charlie from beyond the grave.

Annie is thrilled with this contact to the point of maniacal obsession—but the ritual is not what it seems. Joan and Annie's mother have been in league with a cult, planning to summon Paimon, a demon from hell. The ritual that Joan tricks Annie into performing is the final step in a process that was decades in the making. As the fearful effects of the ritual unfold, Annie's husband, Steve, is immolated, Ellen's decaying corpse is found in the family attic, Annie is possessed and beheads herself, and Peter is fully taken over by the demon, ending up in the tree house surrounded by satanic worshippers.

With a name like "hereditary" and this elaborately deranged plot, it is easy to read this film as a meditation on or spectacle of mental illness. However, this interpretation implies that Annie's problems can be solved through individualized care such as therapy or medication. Instead, I want to argue that as feminists, we should seize on horror films as examples of structural misery—in this case addressing the structure of the family. Only when faults in our social structure are diagnosed, can they be addressed head on.

The references to Greek myth in the film drive this point home. In a discussion about the Greek tragedy *Women of Trachis*, Peter's teacher asks of the protagonist Heracles, "Remember ... he doesn't have a choice. Does that make it more tragic or less tragic than if he has a choice?" A student answers, "I think it's more tragic because if it's all inevitable, then they're all pawns in this horrible, hopeless machine."

In *Hereditary*, the horrible, hopeless machine is the family, and specifically the family as a social unit in the reproduction of capitalism. On this mythic, tragic level, Annie can't simply leave her family or yell at them or cry. Everything must happen at a magnified scale. Her daughter does not just die, she is beheaded. Her son does not simply rebel, he becomes an ancient demon. She does not fight with her husband, she summons a hellish force to burn him alive.

By rooting his horror film in tragedy, director Ari Aster emphasizes that these family relationships aren't freely chosen but are in fact structures non-consensually bound to the characters. This reading provides us with a counternarrative to the delusion that the family can solve all problems if people simply try harder or love more—an idea that lets capitalism off the hook and allows the system to continue relying on the family to provide an impossible amount of support. If we see the family as a tragedy, we understand that no single person can transform the conventions of this structure and instead posit the need for fundamental change.

In *Hereditary* we watch Annie turn into a monster, but what is monstrous about her is that she refuses her prescribed position in the family and consequently has nowhere to go. The film shows the impossibility of this position as she tries to find ways to cope with the grief of losing her mother. When Annie finally seeks help at a support group, she admits that she doesn't feel that it's possible to seek aid from her family and instead does the opposite by shouldering the burden and avoiding putting stress on them: "I just feel like it's all ruined. And then I realize that I am to blame. . . . Not that I am to blame but I am blamed . . ." When a member of the group asks her, "what do you think you feel blamed for?" She can only answer, "I don't know."

To be a mother is to have committed an original sin and to live out one's life in shame and blame. The mother's only path to repentance is a servile life. And even then, she will never be exonerated. Later, when Annie is offered a chance to unload her anger on her son at the dinner table she asks:

> Why would I want to say something so that I can watch
> you sneer at me? . . . All I do is worry and slave and defend
> you and all I get back is that fucking face on your face, so
> full of disdain and resentment. And always so annoyed.

In this scene of a family at the dinner table—scarier than any encounter with a demon—we are made to realize that Peter's failings as a son are not his fault; he can't help "the face on his face."

The family form does not just put impossible pressures on parents but on children as well. The imperative to "cherish" one's mother is an abstract demand that can prevent the development of actual loving relationships. The violence of assimilation into familial forms that serve capitalism can destroy the potential for affection free of these "sneering" forms. As Susan

Ferguson explains, capitalism exerts pressure "for certain (privatized) forms, (disciplining) practices, and (alienated) states of being to emerge." These capitalist modes obstruct the "communal, open-ended, integrated" potential for childhood.[12]

Clearly, children are not born indoctrinated into capitalism's narrow and instrumentalized vision of the world. But sadly, for survival's sake, parents must hamper the creative and generative imaginations of children to ensure they become "useful" members of society, while at the same time fetishizing an abstraction of "childhood." Through disciplining children's perception of the world, parents are required to instill in their children the same sense of impossibility that parents themselves have learned to feel. Escaping this trap requires honesty. *Hereditary's* depiction of the family as tragedy is outlandish and spectacular, but also a step on this journey.

The family in *Hereditary* is not only a tragedy, but also a "satanic death cult," as Sophie Lewis argues. This cult holds up idealized figures of worship and martyrdom to attract followers and sustain its mythic status. In a *Guardian* article, Elaine Glaser breaks this taboo and exposes the secrets of "the cult of the perfect mother," arguing:

> Too often the inevitable downsides of motherhood are hushed up lest young women are "put off". Yet the scraps of honesty that escape the school-gates stiff upper lip have always brought me huge relief. Realism is a political act: it builds solidarity and better conditions.[13]

Although *Hereditary* is far from realism, it is a corrective to the cult of the perfect mother, a relief from Glaser's experience of the ways that motherhood has made her feel: "desperately lonely, existentially bored and excruciatingly humiliated" as her imperfections are thrown in her face. Despite decades of feminism, we haven't faced the exploitation of motherhood

---

12 Susan Ferguson "Children, Childhood and Capitalism: A Social Reproduction Perspective," in *Social Reproduction Theory: Remapping Class, Recentering Oppression*, ed. Tithi Battacharya (London: Pluto Press, 2017), 113.

13 Eliane Glaser, "Parent trap: why the cult of the perfect mother has to end," *The Guardian*, May 18, 2021, https://www.theguardian.com/lifeandstyle/2021/may/18/parent-trap-why-the-cult-of-the-perfect-mother-has-to-end.

head-on, and still cling to unrealistic expectations. Feminists may give lip service to analyzing the oppression of domestic work, yet, as Glaser writes, "mothers are still underpaid, overworked, exploited, overlooked, frazzled, isolated and perpetually guilty."

If we deny the tragedy of the family in the present, Sophie Lewis suggests, we will obscure the potential for a transformed future. Recognition of the instrumentalized, constraining roles of the family has to happen before we can imagine what liberation would look like. Perhaps a future "happy family" won't be a family at all. If we do still have recognizable families, they must at least be optional. But as it stands family membership is mandatory. Lewis argues, "the central fact about Annie . . . is that she's an unwilling parent."[14] But she can only name this unwillingness in dreams, like when she discloses the pressure she felt to give birth to her son: "I was scared. I didn't feel like a mother. But she [Annie's mother, Ellen] pressured me," only to wake up from this confession having admitted nothing in the waking world.

The structural flaws of the family form are classically depicted in the gothic haunted house film and *Hereditary* is no exception. In addition to the Graham family's darkened forest home, the film is populated with miniature haunted houses of Annie's making. As Nina K. Martin notes, the heroines of haunted house films are subjectively linked with the homes they inhabit. As both a place of protection and threat, these homes become a "psychological labyrinth of confusion and fear" where "madness surrounds the female protagonist like a noxious cloud, following her from room to room, and space to space."[15] The house is not simply supernatural or mystical but rather is the locus of "a truth that has to be symptomatically worked out," as Barry Curtis argues.[16] In this sense, the unrealistic aspects of the haunted house film are themselves a form of realism, which bring "mundane domestic details" into focus "by their spectral inflection." These places of shelter

---

14 Sophie Lewis, "The Satanic Death Cult is Real," *Commune*, August 28, 2019, https://communemag.com/the-satanic-death-cult-is-real/.

15 Nina K. Martin, "Fractured Heroines, Traumatic Pasts: Traversing the Haunted Homes of Horror," in *Horror Comes Home*, ed. Cynthia J. Miller and A. Bowdoin Van Riper (Jefferson, NC: McFarland & Company, 2019).

16 Barry Curtis, *Dark Places: The Haunted House in Film* (London: Reaktion Books, 2009).

are "made strange in order to reveal what is troubling them."[17] The haunted house film strips away the veneer of the "happy house" so that we may face the patriarchal and class-based ideologies that construct this space.

Hereditary both cites and ironizes the long tradition of haunted house films by populating its family home with multiple miniature homes and institutional buildings, drawing attention to the house as a thematic center of the plot. But it also does so through humorously citing the cheesiest conventions of the genre. When Annie is summoning the spirit of her dead daughter she uses a Ouija board, glasses slide on the table, glowing balls float through the house, furniture moves, light fixtures explode. These cliches are sillier than they are scary, displaying both an attachment to and distance from the haunted house genre. Part of the reason for this distance from the traditional haunted house movie is that Annie is not a traditional housewife, trapped in her home. Instead, she is a woman who works two shifts at home, both performing domestic chores and working as a waged artist. While Sophie Lewis argues that Annie's suffering is partly due to her desire to be an artist rather than a mother, I think that we can see her career as another source of pain that is coextensive with her frustration as a mother.

Even though Annie is privileged to make her living as an artist, she is still terrorized by feminized labor in her paid job as well as her unpaid work as a mother. In her book *Work Won't Love You Back*, Sarah Jaffe explains how the job of making art is work that can be exploited, but that this is disguised by its reputation as a kind of sacred and idealized creativity. Under capitalism, she argues, one can compare the "romantic attachment" between an artist and their work to "the familial love women are supposed to have for caring work." Together, these myths "make up the labor-of-love narrative that shapes our perception of work today."[18]

Annie's art shows the continuity between the "labor of love" in the home and the workplace. While the film begins by showing one of her more traditional, domestic dollhouses and blurring this with the house she and her family actually live in, we later see her create models of other sites of

---

17 Ibid.

18 Sarah Jaffe, *Work Won't Love You Back: How Devotion to Our Jobs Keeps Us Exploited, Exhausted, and Alone* (New York: Bold Type Books, 2021), 180.

feminized social reproduction—schools, hospitals, funeral homes. Like the homes she creates, these spaces are not depicted as warm and supportive, but cold, objective, and uncanny. These spaces seem to be Annie's attempt to pin down what is missing from her life and world. She not only refuses her role as wife and mother; she refuses an entire society built on flawed systems of reproductive labor.

Annie's job seems idyllic, but it does not liberate her. Even as an artist, she is still not free to grieve or "strike" from the emotions and repressions demanded of a feminized worker. This is illustrated by the chipper phone calls she receives from a gallery where she is supposed to be showing her work (voiced by the director Ari Aster, who may be here ironizing his own position as a high-prestige worker in the culture industry.) These nagging messages reminding her of her deadlines are phrased as if they are simply the concerned check-ins of a supportive friend, but they don't offer any real intimacy. At one point the gallery owner lets her know that he remembers that she is mourning her mother and daughter and that she is in his "thoughts and prayers," showing the hollowness of his condolences. Even if Annie were to become a full-time artist she would not be free. "A romanticized image of the artist's oppositional work" has become generalized, Sarah Brouillette argues, and through this generalization, the "freedom" of the artist can become commodified, just another form of value-generating work.[19]

The moment when Annie goes on full strike is not simply when she gives up her place as a mother, but when she destroys her miniatures and effectively quits her job. She does this before she erupts into full madness, rampaging through her workshop and leaving chaos in her wake. After this, she is truly "free." But of course, in the genre of horror, freedom means a detachment from reality—that is, full-blown madness.

When Annie effectively tells the universe to "take this job (of mothering, of working, of caring) and shove it" she is liberated from emotional suffering, from painful relationships, and even from the burden of personality. But this liberation is most definitely not a happy ending. Instead, with Annie's entrance into full madness, the film generically shifts from a family

---

19 Sarah Brouillette, *Literature and the Creative Economy* (Stanford: Stanford University Press, 2014), 53.

melodrama to a genre so over-the-top and horrific that it could be a comedy. After Annie's husband is burnt alive, her face seems to drain of all its humanity. She climbs the walls, chases Peter into an attic that contains her rotting mother, and finally saws her own head off as naked, middle-aged Satanists look on. If we go back to the title of the film, *Hereditary*, we might read this fantastic ending as Annie's inheritance of her mother's mental illness. But we might also look at this dissociation from the family as a refusal of inheritance. By the end of the film Annie doesn't have a family, a job, or even a head. There is no question, she is no longer required to participate in the horrible, hopeless machine of the capitalist family.

The Babadook: Possession as Care Strike

Outside of horror, the idea of the family as a "horrible hopeless machine" is unthinkable. In conventional narratives, the family is the opposite of a machine, it is an organic and natural entity, the source of a mother's instinctual pride and joy. But in horror films, such as *The Babadook*, demonic possession allows the "natural" caregiver to express her unruly emotions and needs. While women's reproductive labor is widely seen as a spontaneous, free resource, *The Babadook* shows that every moment of care work comes at a price. The price for the protagonist, Amelia, is repression. In order to *appear* as an instinctive caregiver, she must subdue her needs for romantic love, for sex, for friendship, for creativity, and even for sleep. But guess who doesn't need to repress these desires? The Ba-ba Dook-Dook-DOOK!

The film opens with Amelia tossing and turning in bed as her son, Samuel, thrashes around beside her, keeping her awake. We learn that Samuel is a troubled child, obsessed with monsters. He spends his time practicing magic and building weapons in hopes of warding off his fears. Granted, this child was born out of trauma after his father died in a car cash when he drove Amelia to the hospital while she was in labor. The simultaneous loss of her husband and birth of her child makes it difficult for Amelia to love her son, but this trauma also serves to distance us from the supposed *natural* love that a mother *always* has for her offspring. Samuel is constantly begging his mother to look at him. But sometimes she just can't. Mostly, she speaks to him with a sweet voice but other times her tone veers into anger or disgust, revealing the taboo frustrations of motherhood.

Beyond this grief, Amelia is on her own when it comes to bare survival. In her world, as in ours, there are few supports for a single, working-class mother. The school Samuel attends responds to his behavioral problems by ostracizing him and sending him home. When Samuel can no longer go to school, Amelia is confronted with unsympathetic social workers. Once we get to the overt horror of the film, and mother and son are stalked by a terrifying monster called the Babadook, they can neither find psychiatric help nor get assistance from the police. The only aid available to Amelia is sedatives that quiet and sicken Samuel. In short, Amelia is still responsible for all the reproductive labor required by the nuclear family, but she has to do it alone, with the social safety net of the Fordist era nowhere to be found.

Amelia's impossible position as a single mother is a symptom of what Melinda Cooper calls contemporary "family values." Since the 1970s, there has been a kind of conspiracy to blame single mothers for their difficulties and to deny them the resources that they need. Conservatives blame social and financial crises on poor and racialized people who had children out of wedlock. They claim that this constituency has infected the general population with the disease of "fatherlessness" and selfish reliance on the welfare state. Meanwhile, neoliberals talk a good game of "multiculturalism," but still function as economic vampires, making money on the debt and imprisonment of poor single mothers who are no longer protected by the family wage. Like red and green M&Ms, conservatives and neoliberals may appear different, but inside they are both junk food, idealizing "the family" as a privatized form of support while siphoning off public resources.

Amelia's possession may seem to exaggerate this horror, but the invisible suffering of poor, single mothers is properly terrifying. During the pandemic I got a heartbreaking glimpse into this world as I sat (on Zoom) with students who were considering dropping my class. Many of them were young, poor mothers who couldn't keep the tears from their eyes as they described their dilemma. They had worked so hard to become the first in their family to go to college, but all of their support had been ripped from them during the pandemic. Any hope for childcare was gone, and many of them were fired or forced to quit jobs that had given them a feeling of independence. They were now full-time caregivers and homeschoolers to their children, with no time to study. To top it all off, they had to pretend to be *happy* about it. If they did not tend to their children carefully, they *knew* what would happen—judgement, ostracism, perhaps even jail. Where is the help for these young women? Who cares for the caregivers? How can we pretend to elevate the natural, nurturing role of the mother who gives so much to our society while giving back nothing but punishment and blame?

These questions are made explicit in *The Babadook* during a scene where Amelia has reached her breaking point. Watching TV during a sleepless night, she sees a crime scene in which a Black woman is dragged out of her tenement housing by cops after having murdered her own son. In the window of this decrepit building, Amelia sees her own haggard face. Here, the comparison is explicit. Single, working-class mothers are expected to both uphold the family and take the blame for its failures.

Not only is Amelia abandoned in her quest to parent alone, but her work life is also unfulfilling and unsustainable. The double burden of care work at home and at work is signified by Amelia's clothing. The white nightgown she wears at home evokes the classic horror film *Nosferatu*, in which female victims are visited at night by an expressionist vampire whose appearance is in many ways similar to that of the Babadook. Following the gothic themes of *Nosferatu*, in her white nightgown Amelia represents an always imperiled domesticity, as she is beset by a male predator and by her own desires. In this formulation, she is expected to be a chaste, obedient, and caring domestic figure. But, as in *Nosferatu*, Amelia's encounter with the monster unleashes her bloodlust. In this, she is both victim and enemy, symbol of endangered purity and violator of gendered categories.

At her job, too, her clothing represents her relation to her gendered exploitation. Wearing a pink dress, she performs care and patience, constantly adapting to the needs of her boss and wards. This care work typically attributed to women is often referred to as "pink collar" work that takes its cues from the domestic sphere, naturalizing and undervaluing "women's work." Amelia rises to the occasion, patiently catering to the whims of the elderly residents, but when she requests some flexibility from her job to tend to her son or her own health, her bosses are harsh and unforgiving, cutting her shifts, evoking the question again—who cares for the caregivers?

Amelia's life reflects the "crisis of care" in our contemporary moment, which has only worsened during the COVID-19 pandemic. Nursing homes are characterized by impossibly long hours, lack of personal protective equipment, chronic staffing shortages, and low wages. In the US, the mean hourly wage for assisted facility worker is $13.36 an hour and the average annual salary is $27,790, which is at the poverty line for a four-person family.[20] As care worker Shatonia Jackson so pithily puts it: "Why do people not respect nursing home and home care workers? People think because you clean shit, you are shit, but if nobody cleaned up the shit, the world would be full of shit."[21] On top of cleaning shit, nursing home workers are required to be loving and patient, even when facilities are so understaffed that they barely have time to feed residents. When they inevitably fail, they are demonized and made to feel like "monsters," a feeling that *The Babadook* literalizes.

As Amelia reaches the end of her patience with both her domestic and work life, Samuel brings her a book called *The Babadook*, which features a shadowy, elongated monster, wearing a top hat and coat. At first this appears to be a children's book with pop-ups and cute rhymes, but its creepy illustrations soon become terrifying when the monster threatens the reader and demands, while lurking over the bed of a sleeping boy, to "let me in!" When Amelia tries to shred the book and throw it away, it shows up on her doorstep with new illustrations that appear to be Amelia killing her dog and her son—"you start to change when I get in. The Babadook right under your skin."

Samuel becomes obsessed with the monstrous Babadook, and his consequent troubled behavior gets him kicked out of school and estranged from the little familial support that mother and child have left. With her job threatened and no social assistance, the sleep-deprived Amelia finally does become fully possessed by the Babadook.

---

20 "Occupational Employment and Wage Statistics," *U.S. Bureau of Labor Statistics*, June 3, 2021, https://www.bls.gov/oes/current/oes311120.htm.
21 Michael Sainato, "US workers who risked their lives to care for elderly demand change," *The Guardian*, April 19, 2021, https://www.theguardian.com/us-news/2021/apr/19/nursing-home-care-workers-coronavirus.

At first the monster seems to be haunting the house, the symbol of the family and "hearth of darkness," as Tony Williams puts it. During sleepless nights, Amelia hears metal scraping, doors creaking, insects chittering, scratching, moaning, and growling. As time surreally progresses, the Babadook takes its human form and enters Amelia through her screaming mouth. Before her possession Amelia's anger occasionally surfaced, but it was quickly swallowed and dissolved into motherly sweetness. The Babadook unlocks this repression and gives her fury full reign. When Samuel asks to be fed, she replies, in a raspy, cruel tone divorced from her usual gentleness, "If you're that hungry, why don't you go and eat shit." And later she will even admit, in reference to her dead husband, "you don't know how many times I wished you were dead instead of him." This is the uncanny—a monster as intimate and familiar as a mother's love.

Not only is Amelia released from the perpetual emotional labor required of her during this possession, she can also escape a constant weariness. As a care worker who is always on the job, whether it is her first or what Arlie Hochschild calls "the second shift"—the domestic work a person does after their paid job—she is always on call and never her own person. In her face stress intermingles with gentleness, reflecting a life of non-stop repetition and care. The Babadook allows her to express her pain and to escape into other, taboo states—such as rage and ecstasy.

Amelia's pain has been symbolized throughout the film as a toothache that makes her flinch and twitch. Towards the end of the film, as she fully transforms into the Babadook, she (I'm sorry to report) snaps the neck of the family dog. Following this she reaches into her mouth and yanks the offending tooth out. Yes, she has become a monster, but she has also escaped a life of constant affliction.

This possession is grotesque but it also liberating. As Barbara Creed puts it, in horror "possession becomes the excuse for legitimizing a display of aberrant feminine behavior which is depicted as depraved, monstrous, abject—and perversely appealing."[22] The possessed woman symbolizes all that society rejects—the unsightly excesses of anger, the disgusting expulsion of impure fluids, the unthinkable extremes of sexuality. But possession

---

22 Barbara Creed, *The Monstrous-Feminine: Film, Feminism, Psychoanalysis* (London: Routledge, 1993), 31.

is also a reclamation of these extremes. The possessed woman is a perverse, rebellious body that is uncontrollable by men. She represents patriarchy's failure to fully contain and manage feminine excess. She refuses the symbolic order as it is. She breaks down every taboo. She may kill her husband, beat her children, masturbate in public—anything goes. The most famed filmic victim of possession, Regan in *The Exorcist*, goes from a sweet "normal" teen girl to a grotesque, howling demon, covered with vomit and piss while spewing obscenities. Possession is not only refusal, it is what Julia Kristeva and Barbara Creed call the power of abjection: "a rebellion of filthy, lustful, carnal, female flesh."[23]

Amelia's possession by the Babadook alters her temperament, making her scary, angry, sexual, and alive in ways she is never allowed to be in her everyday life. It is perhaps this explosive aspect of the Babadook that made it into an unexpected gay icon. As Claire Sisco King argues, a "Babadiscourse" has emerged out of the film that evokes its monstrosity to "call for critical attention to normative constructions of the family, the hegemony of reproductive heterosexuality, and the implications of both for the lives of women."[24]

Coming Out as Babashook

In 2017 the Babadook became a gay pride icon. This initially started as a joke after Netflix accidently listed *The Babadook* as an LGBTQ film, but the idea caught on because of the campy appearance of the monster and the feminist themes of the film, giving rise to "babashook" memes that depicted the Babadook holding rainbow flags and dressed fabulously. As someone on Twitter put it, "openly gay, and with an affinity for hats and drama, the Babadook was the first time I saw myself represented in a film."[25] Or as Karen Tongson explains, "He lives in a basement, he's weird and flamboyant, he's living adjacently to a single mother in this kind of queer kinship

---

23 Ibid, 38.

24 Ibid, 38. "'If It's in A Word': Intersectional Feminism, Precarity, and *The Babadook*," *The Popular Culture Studies Journal*, 6.2–3, (2018), 166.

25 Alex Abad-Santos "How the Babadook became the LGBTQ icon we didn't know we needed," *Vox*, June 25, 2017, https://www.vox.com/explainers/2017/6/9/15757964/gay-babadook-lgbtq.

structure." A gay man interviewed about the significance of the Babadook called it Amelia's "dark, drag persona," which allows her to "finally realize her truth."[26]

In *The Babadook*, along with many of the films I will discuss in this book, we cannot extricate monstrosity and queerness. The challenges these monsters pose to the family, to the naturalness of feminized labor, to feminine compliance, are all threats to heteronormativity, and are thus, in a broad sense, queer. Theorists like Harry Benshoff, Robin Wood, and Michael Bronski have researched the queerness of horror films and their monsters in depth, and once you start looking, you find it everywhere. The hounded monster in *Frankenstein* can be seen as a figure of queer ostracism. The phantom of the opera must hide his unrequited, abjected love. Count Dracula's sexuality is non-procreative, evil, and deadly. Mr. Hyde can be viewed as a dark secret emerging from Dr. Jekyll's closet. Indeed, Harry Benshoff makes a compelling case that monsters are structurally *always* queer:

> Both movie monsters and homosexuals have existed chiefly in shadowy closets, and when they do emerge from these proscribed places into the sunlit world, they cause panic and fear. Their closets uphold and reinforce culturally constructed binaries of gender and sexuality that structure Western thought. To create a bold analogy, monster is to normality as homosexual is to heterosexual.[27]

Queerness is not only a sense of otherness embodied by the monster, but can also be seen in a style of narration that infuses many of the horror movies which interest us here—camp. Camp is characterized by exaggeration and reflexivity; it is a style that is extreme and knowing. This style has been nurtured and developed in queer sociality as a form of self-expression and protection. And even in horror films that are not explicitly queer, we can see camp in the theatricality of the monsters and the storytelling style.

26 "How did the Babadook become the unexpected icon of Pride," *The Irish News*, June 12, 2017, https://www.irishnews.com/magazine/daily/2017/06/12/news/how-did-the-babadook-become-the-unexpected-icon-of-pride-1052661/.

27 Harry M. Benshoff, *Monsters in the Closet: Homosexuality and the Horror Film* (Manchester: Manchester University Press, 1997), 1-2.

Camp is comic, but it also springs from serious desires and fears. As queer novelist and screenwriter Christopher Isherwood said, "you can't camp about something you don't take seriously, for camp requires that you're expressing what's basically serious to you in terms of fun and artifice and elegance."[28] Those who are babashook may be engaged in a playful appropriation, but they are serious about queer liberation.

The seriousness and playfulness of camp is a useful weapon for feminism in that it allows us to grapple with the paradoxes we face. We often genuinely love our family, and yet we are held hostage by that love, which allows others to demand that we endlessly work for free. Most of us crave more love than we are getting, but we don't yet have a language for how that love would work or what it would mean. We want to be useful, but we don't want to be used. We want rewarding work, but under capitalism, we're not sure what that would look like. The campy conclusion of *The Babadook* gives us a glimpse of how to think about these contradictions.

In the end, Amelia emerges from her possession by the Babadook and becomes a loving mother. However, something has shifted. Longings and resentments that could not be spoken before her possession have come to the surface. As feminist journalist and new parent Arwa Mahdawi has recently written in *The Guardian*, "the first rule of Parent Club is that you don't talk about how difficult Parent Club is to the people in Childfree Club. Instead, you smile smugly and say things like: 'You must have a kid, it's amazing!'"[29] Amelia has broken through that taboo, and her final transformation leads us to speculate what would happen if we all allowed ourselves to be "possessed" by our real feelings and expressed them openly. Amelia can no longer deny that parenting is hard work and that emotional labor is unnatural and often painful.

Rather than play by older rules of the genre, this woman-directed contemporary horror film creates new conventions to criticize the repression that comes with the "cult of motherhood." Unlike *The Exorcist,* in which

---

28 Quoted in Fabio Cleto, "Introduction: Queering the Camp," in *Camp: Queer Aesthetics and the Performing Subject,* ed. Fabio Cleto (Edinburgh: Edinburgh University Press, 1999), 28.
29 Arwa Mahdawi, "What do new parents like me really need? The unvarnished truth about babies," *The Guardian,* June 8, 2021, https://www.theguardian.com/commentisfree/2021/jun/08/what-new-parents-really-need-unvarnished-truth-about-babies.

the possessed woman is purged of the demon and order is restored, in *The Babadook* the monster leaves Amelia's body but it sticks around as a camp reminder of ever-lurking fear. From now on she will keep the monster in her basement and feed it regularly (with writhing bowls of worms, no less). The monstrosity of reproductive labor can't be banished and will no longer be invisible. It will be something that mother and son openly and even playfully grapple with as they make their way through the cruelties of their world.

In this ingenious conclusion, feminized care work is exposed as a monster in the basement whose daily feeding ritual never loses its rhythmic periods of shock and terror. And yet, the final image we are left with is Amelia and Samuel holding each other in the sunlight. Both seem to be genuinely enjoying each other's company; for the first time, the tension has drained from Amelia's face. In order to begin to access the love we want, the film seems to conclude, we must speak openly about the trauma, labor, and ideology that prevent us from getting it.

Under the Shadow of Global Capitalist Patriarchy: Housework Writ Large

One of our great feminist "mothers" is Kate Millett, who wrote the book *Sexual Politics* in 1970. In it, she offered a novel reading of heteropatriarchal sexual relations by examining the sexist assumptions in literary works by D.H. Lawrence, Henry Miller, and others. As much as we should admire and continue to read her work, as "Stepford Daughters," we should also criticize and analyze the limits of second-wave feminism. When Millett was invited to Iran to speak on women's issues some years later, her visit reflected an imperialist sensibility cloaked as feminist. Here were her words on spotting veiled women waiting for her at the airport:

> The first sight of them was terrible. Like black birds, like death, like fate, like everything alien. Foreign, dangerous, unfriendly. There were hundreds of them, specters crowding the barrier, waiting on their own. A sea of chadori, the long terrible veil, the full length of it, like a dress descending to the floor, ancient, powerful, annihilating us ...

The women she encountered had been part of a movement to defeat the Pahlavi state, a US backed regime riddled with class and sexual inequality. In that battle, traditional clothing and customs took on complex significa-tion, as leftist and religious forces sought to find a language of liberty and anti-imperialism. Iranian women had been deeply involved in all aspects of the revolution, and now that it had been accomplished, were battling on another front, as they marched together on International Woman's Day to contest the new regime's proposal to make hijabs mandatory for women in the workplace. Millet demonstrated her ignorance by glossing over these nuances in favor of a simplistic liberal-Western feminism in which the veil was seen as nothing but a patriarchal tool of "annihilation."

We should not watch *Under the Shadow*, a Persian-language horror film by Iranian-born director Babak Anvari, with Millett's naivete. Instead, we should attempt to understand it through a feminist lens that is also anti-im-perialist and aware of the role the US plays in oppressing Muslim women. In this familiar tale, depicting a housewife driven mad by her circumstances, the "monster" that haunts our protagonist, Shideh, is both a Djinn—a supernatural being common in Islamic folklore—and wears a *chador*—a full length religious veil. While it would be easy to read this film as an allegory for the effects of oppressive religious fundamentalism, a closer look allows us to tell a more complex story.

Throughout most of the film the viewer is confined to Shideh's apart-ment, where she is constricted by her duties as a housebound mother while her doctor husband is called away to the front of the Iran-Iraq war. The film's horror stems from Shideh's frustration with her role as an abandoned housewife, as well as the bombs raining down on her circumscribed world. Her frustration at oppressive housework is aggravated by the microagres-sions she suffers at the hands of her religious neighbors as well as public codes of modesty and the constant threat of arrest for violating them. On one level, *Under the Shadow* is certainly *about* the entrapment felt by a woman whose society offers no escape from reproductive labor and religious, patri-archal constrictions.

The first scene of the film, however, casts a shadow over this narrative. Here we see Shideh begging a school administrator to allow her to resume her medical studies. He rejects her flatly, not because she is a woman, but because of her activism in the 1979 revolution. Shideh does her best to recant her commitment to leftist idealism and yet, she is stonewalled. Shideh's background as a revolutionary is rarely mentioned for the rest of the film; her silence is the film's silence. But the repression of revolutionary desire does not mean it is gone. It casts a long shadow.

After this scene, Shideh returns home, where she tells her husband of her failure to continue her education. While he seems to commiserate at first, he goes on to suggest that it could all be for the best and that she can now dedicate herself to being a full-time mother and housewife. That frustrating possibility sets her on the road to madness and possession as her family home literally begins to fall apart.

As the tenants of her apartment begin to abandon the building, not only do the bombardments intensify, but Shideh and her daughter Dorsa experience more frequent visitations from a supernatural force, suspected to be a Djinn. Favorite objects disappear, such as Dorsa's doll, Shideh's workout tape, and a medical book given to her by her mother. Finally, the Djinn appears in the form of a floating chador, threatening to encompass and drown both mother and daughter. The pair barely escape, but we see that their totem objects are left behind, meaning that their souls are still in danger.

The conventions of the horror film, such as uncanny doubling, the use of shadow and dream logic, as well as what Barbara Creed calls the "monstrous feminine," are all in play in this film, highlighting the terror of Shideh's devalued work as a housewife. Subjective terror is made palpable as Shideh's family home is shown to be full of cracks that reflect her shattered sense of self. Sometimes the cracks in the ceiling and tape on the windows are explainable by the constant shelling of the building. However, these fissures transform and expand according to Shideh's internal state.

Under the Shadow develops this domestic uncanniness through Dorsa's fixation on her doll, Kimia, which is eventually stolen by the Djinn. As Freud argues in his essay on the uncanny, dolls tap into deep psychological fears, obscuring the line between life and death. As we look at the waxen or vacant-eyed faces of creepy dolls, we wonder "whether a lifeless object might not in fact be animate." But, as surrogate children, dolls also represent the domestic. Dorsa's ragged doll embodies a blurring between love and resentment. The child clings to Kimia as a symbol of nurture and care, but the doll disappears and returns dismembered, signaling both Shideh's ambivalence and Dorsa's fear of abandonment.

This uncanny doubling is not limited to Dorsa's doll. Dorsa too, is doubled. Throughout the film, Shideh's encounters with her daughter are ambiguous. Sometimes Dorsa is flesh and blood, other times she is a dream figure or a figment of Shideh's imagination. In the film's climax, Shideh tries to run away from her haunted apartment, only to find that her daughter is the Djinn in disguise, appearing as a veil with terrifying teeth. This uncanny doubling illustrates the shadow side of mothering, in which the person a woman loves most is also the source of her confinement and resentment.

Shideh's husband also becomes a figure of uncanny doubling. His infrequent calls from the war front are marred by static, preventing any intimate communication, yet they are still a form of connection. As Shideh descends into madness, an accusatory voice that may or may not be her husband is heard through the telephone relaying her worst fears—"You're useless. You're nothing but a disappointment. Even your daughter hates you."

Even Shideh herself is an uncanny doubled figure. The Djinn, taking the form of an unseen woman in a chador, is a version of herself, as we see by Dorsa's confusion when trying to distinguish between the ghost and her mother. This double is an empty husk of material, with no life of her own. And yet when Shideh is failing at mothering, Dorsa prefers the Djinn: "She says you can't look after me, but she can." As with Amelia in *The Babadook*, the Djinn expresses Shideh's taboo emotions. As a giant veil or a monstrous woman, she threatens, slams doors and ultimately tries to absorb and drown mother and child, showing Shideh's repressed aggression and desire to self-destruct, rather than live out the frustrating life of a housewife.

We can read the Djinn as a magical chador that threatens Shideh with a future in which she will never be able to enter the public sphere and where she will be confined to the endless repetition of housework. But we can also look at the Djinn as a more nebulous figure of desire. This takes us back to the first scene of the film, where we learn that Shideh must recant her yearning for a leftist revolutionary politics. Throughout the film there are other hints that although she claims to aspire to be a doctor, this is a cover for a more unspeakable longing. Her husband notes that she was much more interested in revolution than medical training in college, and that she ridiculed him for concentrating on professionalization. Later he confronts her with the fact that being a doctor was really her mother's dream, not her own.

In another telling scene, Shideh takes Dorsa to a doctor (one of her few escapes from the house). The physician is a friend from medical school, who was part of "the old gang." On the surface the two of them have a straightforward conversation about Dorsa's health, but from the few words they do exchange, we see that there is a bond and that he is a sympathetic ear, contrasting her husband. We get the feeling that he was not just a friend but a comrade, the only clue we get of Shideh's lost life as a revolutionary. Implied here too, is that support and love does not come from the nuclear family, but from a social solidarity that we can only dream of.

As Langston Hughes asks in his famed antiracist poem "Harlem," what happens to a dream deferred? In this case we might see it in a mystical, nebulous figure such as a Djinn. We can compare this indeterminate force to what Shahla Talebi describes as the melancholia experienced by Iranian women on the Left. During the revolution, tens of thousands of people perished. Thousands more died as political prisoners following the new regime's consolidation. Talebi tells the story of Mahtab, a woman who spent years in prison for her revolutionary beliefs. When she was finally released, she found herself without goals or aims. Her husband had been killed and her son had forgotten her. Although she tried to make herself useful, tending to the poor as a doctor, without the meaning that revolutionary politics gave to her life, she was no longer able to go on, and committed suicide.

Talebi describes Mahtab and other women's post-revolutionary lives as a horror film or ghost story. Shideh's shattered and cracked apartment echoes Talebi's characterization of life for these women: "It is as though their bodies and souls are covered with thousands of pieces of broken glass that cut deeper each time a new violent incident, or even a joyous moment, touches them."[30] Their smiles are haunted with "the ghosts of the untimely dead." These women must leave behind their unspeakable revolutionary

---

30 Shahla Talebi, "Who is Behind the Name? A Story of Violence, Loss, and Melancholic Surival in Post-revolutionary Iran," *Journal of Middle East Women's Studies*, 7, no. 1, (2011), 42.

passions and enter a world where love and attachments are only offered if they conform to ideals of marriage and motherhood.

Capitalism assigns hierarchical gendered roles everywhere, even if these hierarchies take different forms globally. Yet, as we can see in the discourse around US involvement in the Middle East, a fake kind of feminism has developed to legitimize capitalist, colonizing forces, by imagining that "Western" women are free and Muslim women uniquely suffer from sexist oppression. Arash Davari makes the case that this is part of a larger shift he has seen even amongst formerly revolutionary Iranian emigres. Those disappointed with the aftermath of the revolution often turn from a theory of leftist transformation to one of "human rights," hoping for a way out of politics and ideology. And yet, with this turn, "a range of possible struggles for dignity and justice are rendered illegible—not debated and refuted on points of merit but simply silenced wholesale."[31]

For instance, if we come to believe that women's rights can be established by simply negating religious fundamentalism, we can no longer understand struggles against the US government unless they are also anti-religious. This is a betrayal of people like Shideh, whose formative desires involved a struggle *against* US imperialism and so can't possibly be rescued by their enemy. A clinging to secularism and the imagination of "human rights" as the new political ideal obscures the reality that war and imperialism are advanced under the guise of liberalism and human rights. Shideh does not simply need to defeat fundamentalism, she needs access to her former dreams—as a revolutionary she wanted to be an autonomous woman, but she also wanted freedom from capitalism. Secularism alone will not solve her problems.

It seems that Shideh has been overtaken by this simplistic secular dream, as she clings to her one escape from daily life, a Jane Fonda exercise tape (a forbidden item that she must hide when religious people visit the house). From Shideh's TV set, Jane offers encouragement: "Do it you can do it oh yeah," and "There's so much more to you than meets the eye." This fetish object is perfectly emblematic of Shideh's predicament. Jane

---

31 Arash Davari, "Like 1979 All Over Again: Resisting Left Liberalism Among Iranian Émigrés," in *With Stones In Our Hands: Reflections on Racism, Muslims and U.S. Empire*, ed. Sohail Daulatzai and Junaid Rana (Minneapolis: University of Minnesota Press, 2018), 124.

Fonda once stood for leftist resistance, but in the eighties her image had been coopted by Reaganite individualism and emptied out of political content—turned into the perfected hard body, an aerobics icon for the "me generation."

A critique of individualistic independence is marked by the fate of Shideh's Jane Fonda tape. Initially, the tape helps Shideh blow off steam through its ability to absorb her misery. The first time we see her working out, we hear loud, cheerful music emanating from the TV as Jane encouragingly calls out instructions. Shideh is lost in her exercise, blotting out her husband's accusing stare. The next time, however, when she attempts to escape from the emotional labor of mothering by working out, the sound of the tape gradually fades. What once seemed like an invigorating activity now appears spooky and desperate as we watch Shideh work out in a darkened room, with only the sound of her ragged breath and the whistling wind. Later, the Djinn steals her tape and she must perform her routine from memory while facing a dark screen. Again, we only hear the bleak sound of breath and wind, and Jane's colorful image is replaced on the screen by the distorted reflections of Shideh and Dorsa. Fonda's workout tape is not a symbol of independence but of social depletion. Without other options, it is understandable that Shideh throws herself into this activity. But it offers diminishing returns. Far from liberating, Jane (as a symbol of individualist "feminism") is another step in Shideh's slow slide into madness and possession.

Shideh and Dorsa ultimately escape their cracked and shattered apartment, but their future is far from certain. We have learned earlier that the Djinn holds onto its victims by stealing a precious belonging, and the closing shots of the film show that Dorsa's doll and Shideh's medical book are still trapped in the house with the doomed Djinn. Perhaps this sinister ending was a foregone conclusion in that these items are themselves ambiguous. It is not clear that either the doll—representing individualized caretaking, or the book—representing a career, can provide the answer to a longing that is as nebulous as the ever-present wind blowing through the cracked walls and shattered glass windows of Shideh's bombed-out home. The answer can't be found in the abandoned belongings of the nuclear family, but in a revolutionary solidarity lost in the folds of the Djinn's chador and drowned out by the sighing winds.

The *Dark Water* of Single Motherhood

As we have learned from *Under the Shadow*, the home is no protection from a world of danger and precarity. While we may yearn to see the family home as a warm, safe space, insulated from travails of daily life, its sturdy front belies fragility, cracks, and holes. In *Dark Water*, the home Yoshimi struggles so desperately to build for herself and her daughter, Ikuko, is far from solid. Yellowed moldy stains spread on the ceiling, oily water gathers and drips, one awakens from feverish sleep in a pool of mucky secretions. Nothing can be contained or kept out. In short, home is the place of corrosive, liquified abjection.

As Barbara Creed and Julia Kristeva argue, abjection is key to the gendered politics of horror. Abjection is the feminine—liquified, viscous, flexible, soluble, boundless—that threatens to permeate the masculine—rational, solid, strong, erect. Connecting this concept to social reproduction and labor, Maya Gonzalez and Jeanne Neton refer to the abject as feminized work that is considered worthless: "what cannot be subsumed or is not worth subsuming."[32] Abjection is work that no one cares about, work that leads to a lack of self-worth, internalized by feminized and racialized people who have no choice but to pick up the slack. As the state becomes less willing to pay for social reproduction such as healthcare, infrastructure, and education, the labor needed for care will become more and more abject, devalued, and corrosive.

Dark Water is a Japanese horror film that drips with the viscous fluid of abjection. Indeed, the "monster" of this film is simply water, but water that is a symbol of women's reproductive labor and society's neglect of the infrastructure that would allow this labor to sustain life. The film begins with a shot of a neglected young girl waiting outside her school in the pouring rain. Following this it cuts to Yoshimi at a divorce mediation, learning that her ex-husband plans to sue for custody of their child, Ikuko. It seems to her impossible that he could want this since "up to this point he's never taken care of her, not even once," supporting Ryo Hirayama's point that modern masculinity in Japan requires "not

---

32 Maya Gonzalez and Jeanne Neton, "The Logic of Gender: On the Seperation of Spheres and the Process of Abjection," in *Contemporary Marxist Theory*, ed Anderew Pendakis et al. (London: Bloomsbury, 2014), 169.

merely disregarding the care and support provided by women on which men actually depend, but also denying women personhood."[33] Yoshimi's ex-husband could accept her labor as long as it was invisible, but now that she is claiming independence, he cannot allow her to monopolize care of their daughter.

With the threat of losing custody hanging over her, the pressure is on for Yoshimi to provide a stable home for Ikuko, and she proceeds with determination—finding a kindergarten for her daughter and renting an apartment in a large, unkempt building complex with brutalist architecture. She is in such a hurry to settle down that she ignores the apartment's less savory features, such as an ugly stain on the ceiling and an ominous moment while she is viewing the apartment, when Ikuko temporarily goes missing. After hastily agreeing to rent the decrepit apartment, she must find a job, since she had given up her career when she became a mother and now must try to pick up where she left off six years later.

Miraculously, Yoshimi does get a job, but it monopolizes her time, making it difficult for her to pick up Ikuko from kindergarten. Meanwhile, spooky things begin to happen at the apartment building. Ikuko finds a child's red backpack on the roof, which Yoshimi insists she put in the lost and found. And yet it appears on the roof again and again, even when Yoshimi throws it away. Ikuko continues to be drawn away to the roof or the apartment above, making her mother frantic. When Yoshimi is riding an elevator alone, the apartment's surveillance screen shows a murky form standing next to her. Worst of all, the mark on the ceiling of the apartment is spreading—a mossy, yellow stain that forms beads of water and drips dark water on mother and child. When Yoshimi calls the building owner and the superintendent to fix the problem, they ignore her or pass the buck.

The filthy, pervasive water terrifies Yoshimi. Yet when she touches it, she feels more than just revulsion. Instead, the water is revealed as a means of transmitting knowledge. While at her daughter's kindergarten, she had previously found out that Mitsuko, a girl Ikuko's age, had gone missing,

33 Ryo Hirayama, "Counting on women while not counting women's personhood: a critical analysis of the masculine ideal of self-made in Japan," in *Routledge Handbook of East Asian Gender Studies* (London: Routledge, 2020), 339.

wearing a yellow raincoat and holding a red bag. She begins to suspect, through this strangely communicating water, that the little missing girl is connected to the uncanny things happening to her and her daughter. The kindergarten principal assumes that the girl was kidnapped by "some perverted individual." But through the osmosis of abject water Yoshimi learns the truth.

When Ikuko becomes ill Yoshimi brings her home and falls asleep crouching next to her daughter. While they sleep, water drips onto them, affecting Yoshimi's dream. In this vision, shot with hazy filters and gothic, askew, canted angels, Yoshimi sees the missing girl, Mitsuko, waiting after school for a parent that never comes (as Yoshimi herself often did as a child, and as her daughter must when Yoshimi can't get away from work on time.) We see Mitsuko, with her red backpack and yellow hooded rain jacket, slowly walking home, to the same building where Yoshimi lives. From this Yoshimi begins to suspect that it is Mitsuko who is haunting mother and daughter.

Later, when Ikuko is once again drawn to the rooftop, Yoshimi follows her and is drawn to a water tank that leaks rivulets of soiled water. This time, rather than run away or try to fix it, Yoshimi connects with the water, letting it communicate a vision to her. She sees a continuation of the day Mitsuko went missing. Abandoned and at loose ends, she drifted to the roof and climbed the water tank, accidentally dropping her backpack in. While reaching to retrieve it, she fell in. Backing away from the tank, a look of shock spreads on Yoshimi's face. She now knows everything. Mitsuko's corpse is in the water tank. Desperate pounding comes from inside the tank, forming tiny fist-like metal mounds. The abject water is not just disgusting waste, it is a vessel of knowledge about the ways capitalism throws away its children, rather than provide them care.

As Yoshimi knows, Mitsuko's disappearance was two years ago. When she looks at the maintenance record of cleaning out the water tank, she sees that it has not been cleaned since then. This water tank, the agent of Mitsuko's death, is what could be called "the hidden abode of social reproduction"—a city's infrastructure allowed to decay, through neglect and carelessness of a society that claims to care about "family values" while making the reproduction of life impossible. This is one point of Melinda Cooper's important book *Family Values,* that shows how neoliberalism is structured by a discourse that claims to cherish families, but that this concern is really a means to blame single mothers for their own poverty and social decay, rather than develop a secure and supportive society.

In *Dark Water,* this neglect penetrates every element of the home. While Yoshimi wrestles with ghosts on the roof, Ikuko is attacked by domestic fixtures. When she tries to get a glass of water, a bathroom sink spits gunked masses of hair at her. She is drawn to a bath that overflows with brown slopping water, spewing aggressive bubbles and finally forming into muddy hands which attempt to strangle Ikuko. While we could blame Mitsuko's ghost, we can also look to the societal neglect that killed her, from a culture of enforced poverty to the austerity and abandonment that leads to forsaken infrastructure.

The disappearance of Mitsuko, then, was not a case of "stranger danger," it was due to the unbearable strains on the family in combination with a lack of state support for infrastructure and social reproduction. While this is a global trend, every region deserves to be examined for its particular position in the global crisis of social reproduction. Prejudice and stereotypical thinking in the US often leads to a logic that dismisses sexism in Asian cultures as "traditional," but we should understand that under a regime of global capitalism, gender and gendered oppression is never simply a cultural difference, it is always linked to capitalist modernity. As Emiko Ochiai argues, Asian gender formations and social reproduction need to be seen through the lens of "multiple modernities," rather than any notion of traditionalism. Many current conceptions of the "good wife and wise mother" were shaped in response to European models.[34] Later, Japan and other Asian countries would "traditionalize" these gender roles as state-building and "cultural geopolitics" demanded responses to and resistance from the west. As this gave way to constructions of the nuclear family along western lines, women became isolated "losing *sociabilité* and kinship ties."[35] That is, the seemingly "traditional" role of the Japanese housewife is really a capitalist identity, one that tears people away from the collectivity of extended families.

34   Emiko Ochiai, "The logic of gender construction in Asian modernities," in *Routledge Handbook of East Asian Gender Studies* (London: Routledge, 2020), 17.
35   Ochiai, "The logic of gender construction in Asian modernities," 19.

When women drop out of the nuclear family, however, things get worse. Women in Japan earn 73 percent of what men earn. Yuko Tamiya notes that conditions are much poorer for single mothers, and their numbers are increasing.[36] Japanese women tend to quit work when they have young children, with only 38 percent of mothers continuing employment after childbirth, but they often try to find employment again once their children can go to school.[37] As in Yoshimi's situation, this makes it harder to find work that provides enough to support a child while allowing the flexibility to accommodate child-rearing.

The statistics bear out Yoshimi's impossible position of trying to work and care for her child. As Tamiya demonstrates, working single mothers in Japan can usually only spare 1.5 hours for childcare per day.[38] This generality is depicted in *Dark Water* by the motif of a lone child waiting outside a kindergarten as happy families slowly drift off and she is finally left abandoned in the dark. This is seen over and over in the film, and the three main characters Yoshimi, Ikuko, and Mitsuko, have their lives defined by the experience. Even with these long work hours, 55 percent of lone parents in Japan live in poverty, reflected in Yoshimi's lack of options, such as the decrepit, leaky building where she must live, whose infrastructural neglect will ultimately kill her.[39] As is the case of single mothers in the US, such systemic obstacles are ignored, while women are blamed. When Ikuko has trouble at school, her principal blames her broken home, criticizing Yoshimi's tendency to pick up Ikuko late. He compares Ikuko to the missing Mitsuko, whose mother mysteriously disappeared, inferring that maternal neglect is at the heart of childrens' suffering, when clearly societal abandonment is responsible. Anne Allison discusses the real-life gothic tales of people left behind by Japan's rising precarity, such as the case of Shimomura, a single mother who flailed as she struggled to care for her two children with few resources and no childcare. Nineteen days after she left home for a last-resort

---

36 Yuko Tamiya, "Lone mother households and poverty in Japan: new social risks, the social security system and labor market," in *Routledge Handbook of East Asian Gender Studies* (London: Routledge, 2020), 254.

37 Tamiya, "Lone mother handholds and poverty in Japan," 255.

38 Tamiya, "Lone mother handholds and poverty in Japan," 258.

39 Tamiya, "Lone mother handholds and poverty in Japan," 259.

vacation, her children were found abandoned and dead in her unregistered apartment. When "selfless, cheerful, compassionate" Shimizu Yukiko, "the perfect daughter" and "consummate caregiver," ran out of resources to tend to her ailing mother, she opted for a double suicide staged at her father's graveside. Only Shimizu died and her mother, in worsened condition, was found "having spent the night in a blinding rain before being discovered the following morning."[40]

Yoshimi is ultimately forced to martyr herself for Ikuko's survival, agreeing to become the caretaker for Mitsuko's spirit so the dead child will not kill her own daughter. In this gesture Yoshimi transforms into pure abjection. As she attempts to flee the apartment, she carries what she thinks is her own daughter, but turns out to be Mitsuko. As the real Ikuko helplessly watches, the elevator doors close on her mother, with dead, mud-caked Mitsuko clinging to her. Ikuko rushes to meet the elevator on another floor, but when the doors open, the chamber emits only a torrent of filthy "dark water." Her mother has transformed into liquified abjection, splashing out over her sobbing daughter.

In my mind, this scene brilliantly and uncannily captures the abjection that besets single mothers and therefore should have ended the film. But the pressures to individualize social problems are strong, and this can be seen in the film's coda. Ten years later, Ikuko returns to the now abandoned apartment building for the first time since her mother's dissolution. There, she encounters her mother in human form, claiming to be "happy" as long as Ikuko is with her. At first Ikuko wishes to return to living with her, but soon she realizes the nature of Yoshimi's sacrifice as Mitsuko's ghost looms behind her. She perceives that Yoshimi has been protecting her biological daughter by assuaging the dead girl, immuring herself as Mitsuko's eternal ghost mother. Yoshimi achieves the sacrifice in death that she couldn't enact in life. This "happy ending" individually "solves" the problem Yoshimi faced by idealizing the figure of the martyred mother, rather than forcing us to grapple with the ongoing

---

40 Anne Allison, *Precarious Japan* (Durham: Duke University Press, 2013), 41–42.

structural abjection that pervades the rest of the film. But these forms of closure can't contain the insistent dark water that seeps through the cracks.

Conclusion: The Unhappiness of the Katakuris

Perhaps Yoshimi is happy in her death. But this only goes to show that under an enforced regime of "family values," the word happiness has lost its meaning. The Japanese horror-comedy-musical film *The Happiness of the Katakuris* follows a family who, after the breadwinner is fired from his job as a shoe salesman, decides to pursue happiness by moving out to the country and immersing themselves in a vigorous, nurturing family life. Like many families in our independence and individualism-obsessed society, they imagine that the path to autonomy and vitality is to start their own business.

Deep in the logic of entrepreneurialism, they are convinced that if they stay positive and optimistic they are bound to overcome all obstacles and achieve their dreams. They open an inn in an area where a new road is slated to be built. With this new development comes the hope for a life of intimacy and prosperity. As they sing to their reluctant teenage son Masayuki: "Let's live here/Let's start here/There's a big new road coming/Will it bring happiness?/Happiness is made by the whole family." Instead of seeking joy from closeness and solidarity, the family's hope lies in a "big new road" which they hope will bring commerce but will only lead to their own ruin.

The family lives in the inn, blending family life and paid occupation, and giving their all to both. But no matter how much cheerfulness and grit they summon, nothing goes their way. Their first guest commits suicide and their next guests, a Sumo Wrestler and a clearly underage girl whom the family fails to protect, perish as well (he has a heart attack during sex and crushes her). From there, the bodies continue to pile up, until finally a volcano behind their inn/home erupts and douses steaming lava onto the family. In a group effort, the Katakuris lift their house above the destruction and avoid catastrophe, but soon after, the oldest member of their family dies and floats to heaven.

Through all these tribulations, the family commits to togetherness and self-help, frequently bursting into songs with lyrics like: "Look on the bright side /

Ok always be positive ok / You can even stop / But always get moving again / Even if no one is waiting for you." These uplifting lyrics support the logic of motivational talks, but the surrealism of this horror comedy makes it known that to "always be positive" is not enough, families need support and security.

As with many other families in this chapter, the problem with the Katakuris is not that they don't care for each other. In fact, through song, dance, forgiveness, and sacrifice, the family consistently displays solidarity and support. Even though this movie is deeply goofy (and intended to be so), we are truly moved when husband and wife Masao and Terue sing to each other: "Your gentle true heart is my solace /Our true gentle hearts are our solace." But the song goes on: "No promotion, no money / All I have is my health." In this addendum, the film contains a message that no matter how loving the people in a family are, they can't escape the economic oppression of the family form.

This is more proof that family abolition is not concerned with denying the real bonds that can form between people as they exist in the family. Many of us feminist radicals love our moms, and rightly so! What is preventing the true happiness of the Katakuris is a lack of structures to *support* the love they covet so deeply. The Katakuris can't simply enjoy each other as family, since the family *form* bears the responsibility for so much more than just love. The family must also sustain itself materially, and *The Happiness of the Katakuris* literalizes the fact that in a world of capitalist competition this means that love can only be built on a pile of dead bodies. In the end we see the family rollicking through green bucolic hills, as if they were in *The Sound of Music* (another film whose innocence is suspect). But despite their pollyanna glee, the happiness of the Katakuris is built on corpses. No matter how loud they sing— "Let's laugh / Leave your sadness to the wind / Tomorrow will be fine / We're all well / Let's laugh together/That's happiness"—a whiff of death infuses the bright spring air.

Like the other films discussed in this chapter, The *Happiness of the Katakuris* shows the family as both a source of horror and an emblem of wider societal perils. Only by becoming monsters or warriors can the protagonists of these films protect themselves from the structures that would naturalize and exploit their reproductive labor until they finally disappear. Whereas conventional realistic or romantic comedy narratives depict reconciliation to these conditions as inevitable, livable, or even heroic and pleasurable, horror provides a space and a language to burn it all down in volcanic ash and perhaps imagine something new in its place.

CHAPTER TWO

IT'S COMING FROM INSIDE THE BOSS'S HOUSE:
HORROR AND WAGED DOMESTIC WORK

Here are some ideas I have for the scariest horror film ever:

A woman is filmed clinging to the window ledge of the apartment she cleans. It is seven stories up. She calls out to her employer for help: "Hold me, hold me." The employer does not put down the camera. She merely films, laughing.[1]

Three children see their mother migrate to a wealthy country in order to support them. They do not hear from her for two years. Finally, her body is found in the freezer of an abandoned apartment.[2]

A housekeeper becomes partially deaf after her employer sticks a pair of scissors in her ear.[3]

---

1   Christina Okello, "Ethiopian Maid Video Underscores Middle East Abuse," *rfi*, March 4, 2017, https://www.rfi.fr/en/africa/20170403-ethiopia-maid-kuwait-video-underscore-middle-east-abuse.

2   Amy B. Wang and Ryan Murphy, "How a Maid Found Dead in a Freezer Set Off a Diplomatic Clash Between the Philippines and Kuwait," *Washington Post*, April 3, 2019, https://www.washingtonpost.com/news/worldviews/wp/2018/04/03/how-a-maid-found-dead-in-a-freezer-set-off-a-diplomatic-clash-between-the-philippines-and-kuwait/.

3   Athira Nortajuddin, "Indonesia's Abused Domestic Helpers," *The Asean Post*, February 26, 2020, https://theaseanpost.com/article/indonesias-abused-domestic-helpers.

A woman jumps off her employer's balcony to escape constant torture and abuse. In a recorded interview she says, "They tortured me and I couldn't do anything to save myself. They beat me every day with an electric cable and wrapped my hair around their hands and dragged me around the room. They smashed my head into the walls." The family is never punished, and later the woman returns to work in their home.[4]

These stories are not fiction. They are real-life accounts of women who perform domestic work. Here, again, the horror is coming from inside the house. But for many of the most oppressed people of the world, the horror is not coming from inside one's own house, but rather the house of another family.

The story of the domestic worker is rarely told in horror, and yet, for many, it is a terrifying condition that deserves representation. This form of labor can expose the worker to the worst of all possible worlds, trapping her in a supposedly intimate space that demands her love and dedication while leaving her with even fewer rights and securities than a housewife, who is at least an official member of the family.

Blood and Milk: The Hyperexploitation of Domestic Workers

In general, the film industry prioritizes white, first-world feminism, leaving the hyperexploited housekeeper invisible. This problem is glaring in the most well-known feminist horror film, *The Stepford Wives*. Here, middle-class white women who yearn for independence are turned into robots who live only to cook, clean, and service their husbands. This scenario is truly horrific, and illustrates the justified fear held by women who want to resist becoming subsumed by marriage and motherhood. But casually dropped into this iconic film is the racist, classist notion that the solution to women's struggles would be to get a maid. With this unfortunate turn in an otherwise powerful, feminist horror film, we learn a lot about *which* women Hollywood believes deserve empathy and protection.

4 Florence Massena, "Abused Ethiopean Domestic Worker is 'The Poster Girl for Kafala' in Lebanon," *Equal Times*, May 22, 2018, https://www.equaltimes.org/abused-ethiopian-domestic-worker#.YMe7fS2cY__U.

In fact, some women have taken this route out of servitude, gaining liberation by supporting the restructuring of domestic work on the backs of poor women of color. As many have argued, our moment is characterized by an international division of labor paired with a gendered division of labor. Productive labor is "feminized,"—that is, it becomes lower waged, less likely to be represented by unions, and more likely to be done by women who are seen to be more controllable and pliable than male workers. Much of this work is sent to the third world as "global care chains" are developed, through which women from poor countries are imported to perform domestic care work.

As Barbara Ehrenreich puts it, "the lifestyles of the First World are made possible by a global transfer of the services associated with a wife's traditional role—childcare, homemaking, and sex—from poor countries to rich ones."[5] At the same time, white middle-class women who employ domestic labor are pressured to appear as if they can manage everything in both their work and home lives. Not only do the women who "have it all" depend on imported workers, they render them invisible to seem to embody these impossible standards. As Arlie Hochschild argues, "when all is said and done, women from both the First World and the Third World are pawns in a far wider-reaching economic game for which they didn't write the rules."[6] Ehrenreich sees this "solution" to a first world "care deficit" as a kind of extractivism, equivalent to extracting agricultural and industrial labor. In this case though, we are extracting love and treating emotional and sexual labor as raw materials to be imported. This raises a further question, is love something that can be extracted?

When considering domestic labor, we fail as feminists if we stop with the image of the middle-class housewife. Angela Davis has criticized the use of the housewife as the archetype of feminized labor. She argues that this ignores the reality that Black women were rarely allowed to occupy this position. Many Black women have been and still are forced to perform waged and unwaged reproductive labor at the same time, much of it is domestic

---

5 Barbara Ehrenreich and Arlie Russell Hochschild, "Introduction," in Barbara Ehrenreich and Arlie Russell Hochschild, eds., *Global Women* (New York: Henry Holt and Co, 2004).
6 Arlie Russell Hochschild, "Love and Gold," in Ehrenreich and Hochschild, eds., *Global Women.*

work for other people. This "double burden of wage labor and housework" must force a reconsideration of the struggles around reproductive labor.

Compounded racism and sexism has meant that Black women and other women of color have had to resist the infinite expansion of their work as they are asked to become "surrogate housewives" and to be underpaid for that undervalued labor.[7] In 1900, for instance, married Black women were five times more likely to work for wages than married white women, and this work was almost exclusively in domestic service and laundering. As Salar Mohandesi and Emma Teitelbaum assert, "the racial segmentation was so stark that in some major cities, as many as 90 percent of wage-earning Black women were domestic workers."[8]

Davis traces the deep degradation of that labor back to the institution of slavery in her essay "The Black Woman's Role in the Community of Slaves." Enslaved women had to undertake all the work of keeping house and mothering without any of the freedom from violence that white slave-owning women were afforded. Davis cites a particularly horrific interview from a former slave who recounts:

> ... women who had sucking children suffered much from their breasts becoming full of milk, the infants' being left at home; they therefore could not keep up with the other hands: I have seen the overseer beat them with raw hide so that the blood and the milk flew mingled from their breasts.[9]

This scene shows the horrific devaluation of Black women's love, as they are made to care for white children while forced to abandon their own. Davis quotes a lullaby sung by enslaved women which shows this abasement, but also reveals a resistant culture that snuck gothic, critical lyrics into a

7 Angela Davis, "The Approaching Obsolescence of Housework," in *Revolutionary Feminism: Communist Intervention Series,* Vol. 3, 363.

8 Salar Mohandesi and Emma Teitelman, "Without Reserves," in *Social Reproduction Theory: Remapping Class, Receentering Oppression,* edited by Tithi Bhattacharya (London: Pluto Press, 2017) 44–45.

9 Angela Davis, "The Black Woman's Role in the Community of Slaves," *The Massachusetts Review,* Vol. 13½, (Winter–Spring 1972): 6.

seemingly soothing song: "Way down yonder in the meadow/There's a poor little Lambie/The bees and the butterflies pickin out his eyes/The poor little thing cries Mammy."[10] The poor little lamb in this song is the singer's own child, who lies abandoned, with the grotesque image of his eyes being plucked from his head, while she is forced to sing to her white boss's progeny. This is the kind of gothic tale of slavery that inspired brilliant Black works of horror fiction such as Toni Morrison's *Beloved*, a novel about a woman who kills her own child to save her from enslavement.

As Evelyn Nakano Glenn argues, women of color have historically been hired as white women's servants, freeing middle-class housewives from drudgery and allowing them to express the finer sentiments of the "fairer sex." In this sense, as my editor Andy Battle commented, "the very notion of a white woman, the shapes of their lives, what they aspire to, was created in part by women of color." To excuse this, women of color were labelled as "uniquely suited for degrading work."[11] Meanwhile, the families of domestic workers were and are ignored and neglected. Black women were reduced to servants and their employers willfully remained blind to the fact that their maids often had children of their own.

In our post-Fordist, post-"family wage" moment, as domestic work becomes increasingly commodified, these divisions persist as "racial-ethnic women are disproportionately employed as service workers in institutional settings to carry out lower level 'public' reproductive labor," while white women assume higher status positions.[12] Even when the direct domination of the household is gone, structural hierarchies replace them, mimicking the hierarchies that characterized domestic work in the home. Nakano Glenn points to the ways that much of this work is disappeared from public sight, behind the walls of nursing homes, chronic care facilities, restaurant kitchens, or in the dead of night as women perform janitorial work in office buildings and hotels. Feminism needs to attend to these complicated relationships so as not to essentialize and universalize the "female experience."

---

10 Davis, "The Black Woman's Role," 9.

11 Evelyn Nakano Glenn, "From Servitude to Service Work: Historical Continuities in the Racial Division of Paid Reproductive Labor," *Signs* 18, no. 1, Autumn 1992, 32.

12   Susan J. Ferguson, *Race, Gender, Sexuality, and Social Class: Dimensions of Inequality* (Newcastle upon Tyne: Sage, 2013), 134.

In the current US context, this domestic work often falls to Latinx women and immigrants. Without these women, households could not function, meals could not be consumed, children could not be raised. Not only do domestic workers reproduce the home, but they also reproduce a fantasy of the American Dream while hierarchies are preserved. Study after study shows that the housework done by women of color and immigrants is badly paid and unpleasant, sometimes going so far as to include abuse or imprisonment. But when we see Latinx domestic workers in popular culture, as Mary Romero claims, maids are turned into mythical figures with "folk wisdom" or oversexed "spitfires" who choose their jobs freely, rather than as modern people suffering from modern abuse.[13] Or, as seen in the recent highly acclaimed film, *Roma*, the domestic worker is depicted as willingly self-sacrificing. Although horror has not often tackled this subject directly, when it does, it can reveal the dark side to the plight of the domestic worker. As we have seen, the horror film's creation of monsters, its use of uncanny and gothic tropes, and its ability to refuse reconciliation or assimilation all contribute to the genre's ability to highlight the terrors that besiege domestic workers as well as the courage with which they fight back.

Bathtubs of Blood: *Housekeeping*

Directed by Jennifer Harrington, the independent film *Housekeeping* tells the story of Lucy, a twenty-five-year-old working-class Latina who becomes entrapped in the job from hell. All her life, she has been motivated to rise above her mother's oppressive conditions as a maid. But familial love for her brother, who is threatened with violence because of his debts, forces her to take any job she can. Lucy pounds the pavement, but is rejected by employer after employer with the repeated refrain on her voicemail: "I'm sorry but you don't . . ." Finally, she reluctantly agrees to work as a maid for three weeks. And while this job will at first seem mundane, it will soon escalate into full-blown terror and torture.

Slowly escalating terror is a convention of the horror genre that helps us understand how everyday tasks and conditions can become horrific

---

13   Mary Romero, "Nanny Diaries and Other Stories: Imagining Immigrant Women's Labor in the Social Reproduction of American Families," *DePaul Law Review* 52, no. 3 (2003): 832.

before we have a chance to do anything about them. Countless horror heroines have had to contend with a situation that begins as odd and mildly upsetting, only to gradually blossom into a full-blown violent and/or supernatural assault. These dramatic scenarios may appear distant from everyday reality. But it is precisely these seemingly over-the-top, unrealistic horror conventions that expose the typical dreadful elements of domestic work, realities that are rarely explored in conventional Hollywood films.

Lucy's first day on the job is ominous. The foreboding feeling is underscored by Lucy's muteness. She is silent, not only in this scene, but for the duration of the film, pointing to the voicelessness and invisibility inherent in domestic labor. Instead of speaking or acting of her own volition she is forced into passivity as she is literally overwritten. Scenes of her working or commuting to work are overlayed by hostile and rejecting notes and voicemail messages from would-be employers and false friends, pointing to the domestic worker's disenfranchisement.

Lucy's invisibility is immediately evident when she first approaches her employer's house. Expecting to be greeted at the door, she instead must let herself into a forbiddingly sterile house that assaults her with a screeching alarm. On the kitchen counter she finds an upbeat letter from her employer, Lindsay Marshall, that outlines her tasks, which are fairly ordinary. One of the requirements of the job however is that she wear a maid uniform. Already, the systemic humiliation is beginning, as she is required to visibly display her low status.

When Lucy returns for her second day, she sees Lindsay has laid out a calendar on which the date she worked is marked by a large red "O." This signifies, a note informs her, that her previous day's work would not be compensated. Not only did Lucy not wear the uniform—a fact Lindsay could only know if she had been secretly surveilling her employee—but the cleaning wasn't adequately done. Using passive-aggressive language, Lindsay informs Lucy that she has placed post-it notes to indicate where the cleaning was deficient. Ominous music plays as Lucy wanders around the spotless house, finding post-it notes *everywhere*. As any rational person would, she storms out and seemingly quits for good. However, when Lucy returns to her apartment, she finds it filled with overturned furniture and pools of blood. This indicates that her brother is being tortured for his debts and that if she doesn't return to work, he may be killed. There is no option but to go back, dressed in the demeaning uniform.

The non-consensual nature of Lucy's work illustrates the conditions of many domestic workers. It may be that in everyday life, the family members of housekeepers are not immediately threatened with execution, but in a world where most families live paycheck to paycheck, the threat of starvation, homelessness, and destitution motivates workers to stay at jobs, even when they are abusive.

The next day she is given only one task, to clean the bathtub. Lindsay has already admonished that Lucy must arrive exactly at nine and work until five on the dot. This means she will scrub the bath for eight solid hours, a gruesomely repetitive task. The monotony of housework is one of the "monsters" in this film, and this is emphasized by the formal approaches to showing Lucy's labors. Her motions are often broken down into a series of stills, appearing as a strobe effect. Here, lack of filmic continuity serves as a formal way to disrupt an ideological narrative depicting this work as smooth, organic, and natural.

At other times we are invited to be bored by the duration of silent scenes while Lucy cleans. These scenes' deliberate slowness demonstrates director Harrington's ability to create experimental techniques that blur the line between low and high genre. Horror is generally associated with trash or mass culture, but the formal and thematic approach of *Housekeeping* and many other contemporary genre films supports Fredric Jameson's point that postmodern culture is characterized by the convergence of elevated and popular forms. In the case of *Housekeeping*, we can detect a continuity with previous waves of politicized experimental film.

As in Chantal Akerman's feminist film that depicts a day in the life of a housewife who is also a sex worker, *Jeanne Dielman*, in *Housekeeping* housework's horror is represented through a kind of "hyperrealism," with long stretches of the film showing Lucy doing repetitive chores. That is, rather than jump scares, the horror in the film is derived from the minutae of everyday toil. In her reading of Akerman's film, Ivone Margulies argues that this focus on reproductive labor is an "antipsychological" mode, implying that the domestic worker's unhappiness is not due to her mental state, but to the conditions imposed on her.[14]

This antipsychological stance is also emphasized in *Housekeeping* by its focus on Lucy's desperate need for money and her employer's strategy of delaying her payment, so that she will endure any horror or abuse in the hopes of later receiving her rightful wage. Lucy's material needs, and the ways that these requirements prevent her from demanding pay from her employer, reflect the general state of migrant domestic workers who may be subject to arbitrary wage deductions, fired without reason, or deprived of pay altogether.[15] Due to the threat of deportation, isolation, unfamiliarity with rights, and the need to support loved ones through remittances, migrant domestic workers rarely feel empowered to demand fair or prompt pay.

Lucy's condition, constructed by the conventions of horror, echoes this helplessness. On her fourth day of work the abuse is escalated when Lucy is commanded again to spend the day cleaning the bathtub. But this time she finds it filled with blood. Instead of fleeing, she briefly wretches and then gets on with the task. The hopelessness of her condition wears her down, and where she was once rebellious, she begins to obey her employer's irrational demands. Her one rebellion is to take off time to attend a mandatory meeting connected to her medical school scholarship. Through surveillance footage, Lucy's brief absence is detected, and she is dealt with severely, first with threats and then with extra tasks that draw her further into violent complicity with her employer.

Lindsay's cruelty is motivated by an elaborate, insane revenge plot—a common motive in horror films—but Lucy's inability to control her work hours or get time off also reflects the general conditions of domestic laborers, who often work fourteen to sixteen hours a day, six days a week, and whose employers may harshly restrict their movements. Like Lucy, who

---

14 Ivone Margulies, *Nothing Happens: Chantel Akerman's Hyperrealist Everyday* (Durham: Duke University Press, 1996), 4.

15 United Nations Human Rights Office of the High Commissioner: "Behind Closed Doors: Protecting and Promoting the Human Rights of Migrant Workers in an Irregular Situation," 2015, https://www.ohchr.org/Documents/Publications/Behind_closed_doors_HR_PUB_15_4_EN.pdf, 26.

spends half her days on public buses, they may be further hampered by lack of access to transportation.[16] These workers testify to horrific punishment for taking back their time, as in the case of Angella Foster, whose employers often forced her to return to perform additional chores after leaving for the day. And yet, when Foster's father died and she had to miss the funeral because of her immigration status, she spiraled into depression. Rather than give her time off to take care of her mental health, the family fired her. Her heart wrenching claims went unheard: "I was dying inside, and you let me go because I was sick."[17]

Just as time theft by employers is rampant, so is surveillance and monitoring of domestic workers. The surveillance used to detect Lucy's absence has become a staple of horror, where found footage and paranoiac imagery often construct the form and content of the genre. But in Lucy's case, we see a real-world correlation in the condition of domestic workers whose "right to privacy is often violated; their correspondence is opened, their telephone calls are monitored, their rooms are searched," as an exhaustive United Nations document reports. This methodical humiliation contributes to a general environment of abuse, "strengthen[ing] the dominant/submissive relationship between employer and the migrant domestic worker" and leading to social and cultural isolation.[18]

The note that Lindsay leaves the day following Lucy's transgression begins: "You Little Whore," and goes on from there, calling Lucy a "little bitch" and referring to her brother as "worthless." The faux friendly tone of the earlier notes is gone. And yet, the missive is still signed off with the symbol for hugs and kisses, pointing to the veneer of friendliness by even the most abusive employers in the age of feminized, emotional labor.

Here again the horror trope of escalating psychological and physical violence echoes real-world conditions for domestic workers, who are especially vulnerable to verbal, psychological, and physical abuse, partially

---

16 Julia Wolfe, "Domestic Workers' Rights in the United States: A Report Prepared for the U.N. Human Rights Committee," *UNC School of Law*, https://law.unc.edu/wp-content/uploads/2019/10/domesticworkersreport.pdf.

17 Carolyn Bick, "Invisible Women: Domestic Workers Underpaid and Abused," *Aljazeera*, October 21, 2017, https://www.aljazeera.com/news/2017/10/21 invisible-women-domestic-workers-underpaid-and-abused.

18 United Nations, "Behind Closed Doors," 19.

because they are hidden away in private households with no one regulating, monitoring, or inspecting their conditions.[19] Made invisible to any protective eye and excluded from laws designed to protect workers, domestic laborers are thrown down stairs, raped, beaten, shouted at, insulted, belittled, deprived of food, and more.[20] The people who perform our most intimate and essential forms of care are seen merely as the deliverers of devalued "women's work," and for this they are left vulnerable to torture.

The pressures on Lucy are not identical to those of a migrant domestic worker, but the claustrophobia and inescapability of her situation gives us insight into this form of entrapment. It is significant that when Lucy appeals to her treacherous friend Denise for advice, she claims Lindsay is just a "nice white lady" who means well. In fact, the threat Lucy's job poses to her is racialized. The source of her terror, the house she cleans, assaults her with its intense whiteness. Rather than finding terror in the shadowy dark, as in the standard horror film, this house displays its monstrosity through its antiseptic, institutional, anonymous *white* glare.

Racial prejudice, of course, is built into the condition of the domestic worker. A 2019 demographic breakdown of US housekeepers shows that only 30 percent were born in the US and only 29 percent were white, while 61 percent are Latinx. The degree to which this profession is gendered is astounding—95 percent of housekeepers identify as women.[21] Even a dry report by the UN Human Rights committee can't help but comment on the politics of these types of demographics: "These intersecting identities often subject domestic workers to significant hardship in a patriarchal and racist American society."[22] Capitalism systematically creates and affirms hierarchies of race and gender to ensure its own reproduction, saving the most intense exploitation for the undocumented and women of color.

While Lindsay's passive-aggressive notes never mention race, her patronizing attitude reeks of white supremacy. She creates infantilizing

19 United Nations, "Behind Closed Doors," 18.
20 United Nations, "Behind Closed Doors," 19.
21 Julia Wolfe, "Domestic Workers are at Risk During the Coronavirus Crisis," *Economic Policy Institute Working Economics Blog*, April 8, 2020, https://www.epi.org/blog/domestic-workers-are-at-risk-during-the-coronavirus-crisis-data-show-most-domestic-workers-are-black-hispanic-or-asian-women/.
22 Wolfe, "Domestic Worker's Rights."

charts and assignments, posting crosses and circles to signify whether Lucy will be paid, virtually playing tic-tac-toe with her life. Ever the patrician pedagogue, she assigns Lucy additional tasks for "extra credit." These patronizing gestures are at one with the ratcheting up of abuse, and this convention of horror— slow escalation—allows us to see the exploitation nestled into seemingly mundane tasks.

Lindsay's initial "extra credit" assignments are bizarre, designed to humiliate Lucy and break down her sense of self-worth. Lucy must catch a fly but not kill it, she must build Ikea furniture with inadequate tools. Next, she receives instructions to "see to the matter in the bathroom." The viewer does not get to see what this "matter" is, but it causes the normally composed Lucy to vomit violently and we later see her dragging a bag across the house that looks like it could be filled with blood and guts. From here, she must enter more deeply into the violence that structures her job by killing the neighbor's cat. By this point Lucy is so broken that she doesn't even bother to protest inwardly.[23] The cat's blood stains her uniform, and where once she kept herself fastidiously neat, she will spend the rest of the film in the unwashed garment. Not only will she neglect her appearance, but her health seems to be affected. Her once brisk step will be replaced by slow trudging, reflecting the illness and accelerated aging that can accompany domestic work as workers are denied access to and information about health care.[24]

It is not only Lucy's health that is eroded, but her dignity as well. In a final move to shred Lucy's ego, Lindsay gives her the task of writing on a mirror: "I am a piece of shit. I do not deserve to live," over and over for eight hours, erasing the words and rewriting them every time the mirror is covered. By now, Lucy must know that this job is nothing but sadism, but she is so broken that she expressionlessly presses on with the task. We can see this experience of humiliation in the everyday realities of domestic workers.

---

23 Many of the films I include in this book include the murder of an animal. This is interesting to think about in relation to reproductive labor. Many feminist theorists have noted that women's labor and women themselves have been seen as "nature." Because of this status, they are considered expendable—outside civilization. In this, they are an extension of the animal and natural world that our society exploits without mercy or penalty.

24 United Nations, "Behind Closed Doors," 21.

As Rokeya Akhatar, a Bangledeshi domestic worker, complained:

> I wasn't allowed to sit at the same table.... I wasn't allowed
> to wash my clothes with their clothes. They made me dif-
> ferent. Sometimes the food I cooked didn't taste good
> to them, and they would yell at me. They made me [feel]
> like. . . they were my owner. [25]

Even when domestic workers aren't exposed to overtly humiliating behavior like this torture, the experience of degradation is frequent, as this difficult labor is diminished as "women's" work, not worthy of legitimation or
protection.[26]

Lucy is not only a victim, she is also a fighter. She shakes loose the
torpor caused by her debasement and investigates her employer, tracking
down Lindsay's true residence. There, she is brutalized but she also learns
the truth of her condition. Upon arriving, Lucy is knocked over the head and
confined to a bedroom. From the room she hears the voices of her brother
and Denise, whose conversation reveals that Lindsay has bribed them to
gaslight Lucy. With the knowledge of this betrayal, the constraints that tethered Lucy to the job are loosened, and she can refuse the emotional labor of
self-sacrifice for family and friendship.

However, even though Lucy has now unlocked the psychological
manacles that tied her to abusive domestic work, she is still materially
constrained. Lindsay's final resort to violence is a reminder that domestic
workers can't always choose to leave abusive conditions, no matter how
informed they may be. We can view the very tangible ropes that bind Lucy
as akin to the material constraints of race and poverty, structural conditions
that can't be willed away.

As Lindsay drives Lucy to an unknown destination, she reveals her
murderous motives. Lindsay is the sister of Alice Goodwin, a young girl
who was killed in the same fire that engulfed Lucy's mother. Lucy's mother
was the maid for the Goodwin family and Lindsay has been punishing Lucy

---

25 United Nations, "Behind Closed Doors."
26 Wolfe, "Domestic Workers Rights."

because, as a child, she ran into the burning building and saved her own brother rather than Lindsay's sister.

This motive seems to stray from the typical power dynamics involved in the abuse of domestic workers, but as Lindsay's monologue progresses, we learn that her resentment goes deeper than the loss of her sister. She relishes insulting Lucy's dead mother and belittling her for her lack of subservience. "Your mom," she says "God, she was always doing shit she wasn't supposed to. She got what she deserved that night." Though Lindsay initially gives off the veneer and tone of an enlightened woman, she means to stay on top, and this extends to keeping generations of Latina women in their place. Rather than revealing herself as a unique psychopath, Lindsay exemplifies how the exploitation of domestic labor is repetitive and adaptive as well as how racial hierarchies must be constantly reinforced.

Finally, Lindsay brings Lucy back to the house that has been the source of her torture, intending to ignite it and leave Lucy to burn to death inside. However, Lucy liberates herself from her bonds and escapes to a new life, free from both Lindsay and her sense of guilt and obligation to her brother and cruel friend. Although Lucy's ordeal has been an illustration of the horror of housework and the ways that domestic workers are victimized by it, in the end she emerges as a warrior rather than a victim. For the entire film she has been voiceless, written and spoken over by words that were not hers, tethered to her abusive job by poverty and familial duty. Now, she triumphantly calls Denise with her own message in her own voice. The words are simple and to the point: "Revenge is a bitch."

To be honest, the ending of this film feels a bit rushed and uninventive. We wish to see Lucy enact more protracted revenge on her torturer and to imagine a broader horizon of solidarity. Instead, we assume that by "revenge," she means that she will go to medical school and forget all about these horrible people, hinting at a belief that one can, after all, pull oneself up by one's bootstraps—in other words, offering an individualist solution to a structural problem.

The shortcomings of this film can serve as a caveat to some of the strong claims I have been making about the political possibilities of the horror genre. It is true that many contemporary horror films are entertaining sources of tools for feminist radicals who want to better understand

and combat oppressive structures. However, the genre has a long way to go before it has adequately tackled some of the most pressing issues of our moment, such as the plight of Latinx domestic workers. Domestic work is performed by millions of feminized people of color and is at the heart of the "crisis of care" that defines contemporary capitalist exploitation, and yet it has inspired only a handful of horror films, most of which are underfunded. Jennifer Harrington's low budget film is a promising beginning, but, in a capital-intensive industry controlled by the bottom line, it will be a long time before we see real representational diversity in the genre.

The Solidarity of Hungry Ghosts in *The Maid*

The Maid is a 2005 Singaporean film that shows the true terror that lies in wait for the migrant domestic worker. As in *Housekeeping*, the horror of working in the intimate, domestic sphere is illustrated by episodes that escalate from the mundane to the explicitly and horrifically violent, as Filipina domestic helper Rosa proceeds from performing everyday tasks in the home to fleeing ghosts at the gates of hell. Worse than these ghosts, though, are the employers who see right through her. By the film's end we learn that while the oppressive bosses are irredeemable, banished and hungry ghosts offer a surprising source of solidarity.

The film begins with the arrival of eighteen-year-old Rosa in Singapore. As a poor, young woman from the Philippines, she is overwhelmed and impressed, "everything was so clean and wonderful." Through panoramic shots of the city, the viewer, with Rosa, is introduced to the modern albeit sterile world that awaits our heroine. Yet something ominous lurks. Rosa's voiceover, narrated from some time in the nebulous future, hints that her present enthusiasm is naïve and near-sighted.

In the opening moments of the film, we have already been warned that something supernatural is afoot. This is the seventh month of the Chinese lunar calendar, or the "hungry ghost" month, a period during which the gates of hell open and the dead return. Soon after Rosa meets her employers, Mr. and Mrs. Teo, they warn her of the dangers of this month, and she witnesses them devoutly erecting their own altar and burning paper money to propitiate the "wandering spirits" of their ancestors.

Rosa is unfazed by this supernatural ambiance and at first her job does not seem too onerous. She cleans throughout the day and her life is limited to the four walls of the Teos' house. But her bosses are polite and she is physically unharmed. We are not particularly alarmed by the tasks that Rosa does—washing dishes, scrubbing, sweeping, preparing breakfast, running errands. But, as is expected in the genre, soon these tasks become horrific. No chore can be done in peace. Ghosts lurk in every corner of the house, jumping out from behind hanging laundry, from cabinet doors, and through crawl spaces. Just as she can never leave her bosses' house, even at night Rosa can't escape the hungry ghosts who haunt her dreams. Yet we don't know what these silent, blank-faced ghosts want.

In her haunted life as a maid, Rosa reflects the life of millions of migrant domestic workers who themselves are ghosts—people who come from another world and who silently and invisibly reproduce tidy houses, cared-for children, and warm meals, enabling the "real" inhabitants of these homes to live comfortably. Filipina women are particularly likely to be doing this work. About one fourth of the 11.5 million people who perform global migrant domestic work are Filipino, and the remittances they send home account for 8.8 percent of the country's GDP.[27]

Yet, despite their huge contributions, domestic workers from the Philippines are excluded from basic worker protection laws.[28] They are often subject to horrific conditions such as "beatings, confiscation of passports, confinement to the home, overlong working hours with no days off, and in some cases, months or years of unpaid wages."[29] These circumstances are horrific and inescapable, as workers are trapped, blackmailed, and intimidated. They are besieged by huge debts incurred in recruitment fees—usually

27 Corine Redfern, "'I want to go home': Filipina domestic workers face exploitative conditions," *The Guardian*, January 27 2021 https://www.theguardian.com/world/2021/jan/27/domestic-workers-philippines-coronavirus-conditions.

28 Kenneth Paul Tan, "Pontianaks, Ghosts and the Possessed: Female Monstrosity and National Anxiety in Singapore Cinema," *Asian Studies Review* 34, no. 2, (2010): 162.

29 "Domestic Workers Convention: Labor Rights Treaty to Take Effect," *Human Rights Watch*, August 6, 2012, https://www.hrw.org/news/2012/08/06/domestic-workers-convention-labor-rights-treaty-take-effect.

the first six months of their salaries are deducted.[30] Deportation lurks around every corner, as their residency is often dependent on the good graces of their employers. Raging winds of misunderstanding lash out at them as they navigate the linguistic and cultural norms of a strange new world. Even love is a kind of damnation as they strive to support and contact family members who are forever receding beyond reach.

Without the visibility that rights and protections afford, migrant domestic workers can become spectral. Because of this connection, it makes sense that Rosa is the only person who can see the spirits haunting Singapore's homes and streets. Her bosses, who are very religious, assume that the ghosts are appearing to Rosa because she has somehow offended them. But it is more likely that Rosa, as a domestic worker, has a sympathetic bond with these banished souls.

Like domestic workers, the ghosts are everywhere, but they are ignored and condemned. This enforced invisibility is echoed in the recommendations employment agencies give to migrant domestic workers. They should appear only as polite service-providers—says an emphatic note by one employment agency, "Be polite and always SMILE. Greet your employer 'GOOD MORNING' 'GOOD NIGHT.' Say 'PLEASE' 'THANK YOU' 'I AM SORRY.'" But they should hide any signs of their humanity—"Avoid crying. It is bad luck to your employer."[31]

It is no wonder only Rosa can see these tears. As Neferti Xina M. Tadiar argues, Filipina maids are often seen as "bodies without subjectivity," not unlike ghosts.[32] She makes the case that these laborers suffer under conditions that are less like free labor than like being a commodity. Migrant domestic helpers can't freely sell their labor power, "rather, their labor power is sold—together with their bodies and their sexuality." Constructed by gender, race, and class, these "commodities" may be called "new-industrial 'slaves.'"[33]

---

30 "Workplace Abuses in Singapore," *Human Rights Watch*, https://www.hrw.org/reports/2005/singapore1205/6.htm.

31 Nicole Constable, "Filipina Workers in Hong Kong Homes," in Ehrenreich and Hochschild, eds., *Global Women*, 147.

32 Neferti Xina M. Tadiar, *Fantasy Production* (Hong Kong: Hong Kong University Press, 2004), 115.

33 Tadiar, *Fantasy Production*, 115.

In assuming that Rosa has offended the ghosts, the Teos are suggesting that she is to blame for her own suffering. In response, they give her instructions on how to adapt to Chinese customs. But this ignores the violence inflicted on Rosa and their own role in it. This is a common way of repressing or ignoring "the violence endemic to the very structure of domestic labor," and instead attributing the problems of domestic migrant workers to "culture shock."[34] As Tadiar argues, this idea covers up the fact that domestic workers are not on equal terms with their employers. The assertion that domestic workers simply need to learn the ways of a different society is a way of saying that these dehumanized workers are simply products "needing further processing before export to other countries."[35]

The problem in the Teo house is not Rosa, nor even the ghosts she sees, but her employers and the system they perpetuate. As the days pass, they tighten their control on her, telling her when and what to eat and preventing her from going out alone, even to send mail to her family. When she is not cleaning or running errands, she must take care of the Teos' developmentally disabled son, Ah Soon, who is generally sweet tempered, but who sometimes erupts into tantrums during which we remember that although he has the mind of a child, he has the threatening body of a large man who has the power to harm Rosa.

Any thoughts Rosa has of leaving the Teos are dashed when she receives a letter from her family letting her know that her brother is very ill and they need the money required to treat him. Her bosses advance Rosa her salary for the full month, for which she is thankful. But now she is trapped, as are so many domestic workers whose families depend on them for survival.

As time passes, Rosa's circumstances become more mystifying. It becomes less and less clear which of the people around her are ghosts and which are real. Ah Soon himself suspiciously evades an accident and later disappears without a trace, only to reappear later just as mysteriously. One ghost in particular keeps returning to Rosa, a young woman in a red dress haunting the rooms of the Teo house. At one point Rosa becomes so afraid that she runs away to the employment agency that hired her. Unsurprisingly, they offer no help, sending her back to the Teos while insisting that she

---

34 Tadiar, *Fantasy Production*, 119.

35 Tadiar, *Fantasy Production*, 119–120.

should be grateful that her "Ma'am" treats her well. Even the most cursory research reveals many cases of Filipina maids in Singapore who were beaten, tortured, raped, starved, and murdered. It is no wonder that the employment agency thinks that Rosa has a good situation.

The ghost in the red dress begins leaving clues for Rosa, revealing herself as Esther Santos. Further investigation finds that Esther was the Teos' previous Filipina maid. Esther never inflicts harm on Rosa but shows her frightening scenarios that hint at the violent circumstances of her own death. But when Rosa confronts Mrs. Teo about Esther, her boss insists that although Esther was a "good girl," she must have met a man and run away as, she asserts, frequently happens with Filipina maids. That is, Mrs. Teo dismisses the possibility that her maid could have been the victim of violence by questioning her morals.

Rosa befriends another migrant domestic worker, Watti, who knew Esther. She insists that Esther had a sick father and needed to send home remittances. She would never have run away. But after revealing this, Watti herself turns into a ghost and leaps to her death. This form of suicide is common and horrifying, driving home the ways these ghosts are really illustrations of the terrors that beset domestic workers, whose lives can become too ghastly for "realistic" representation to do them justice. How can anything but the horror genre depict the conditions for this woman, who attempted suicide and then reported:

> I was afraid if I ran away, I would be caught by the police. Madam often got angry with me, complained to the agency, and the agency also got angry with me. The agent asked "What do you want?" I said, "I want to die, ma'am, because the people here are cruel, everything I do is wrong, I'm always called idiot and stupid."[36]

Like Watti, Esther may be dead, but she can still stand in solidarity with Rosa, helping her to fend off her evil employers. Back at the house, Rosa is drawn to a drum that beats itself and inside this instrument finds Esther's burnt corpse. In the same room, she finds a pile of unsent letters Rosa has

---

36 "Workplace Abuses in Singapore."

been writing to her family. These events trigger another attempt at escape. She dashes out of the house and runs to the mailbox, no longer expecting to live, but at least hoping to preserve her legacy by sending the letters to her family.

Throughout the film, letters to and from her family have been Rosa's one solace. A young mailman has kindly given her stamps, but once Mrs. Teo discovers that Rosa is sending letters, she forbids her to go out on her own, and asserts that she herself will mail Rosa's letters. This scenario reflects abuse in the real world of domestic workers, who are often prevented from writing letters during their work hours or deprived of freedom to leave their workplace. As Nicole Constable argues, "It is as though the employer has bought the domestic worker's labor power and time, not simply hired her to carry out specific tasks."[37]

In Rosa's case, we can see that her employers intend to possess every moment of her time and every inch of her body. This seems to be accomplished as the thin thread that kept Rosa connected to her family and her life is severed. After Rosa is dragged back to her domestic prison the final details of her employers' deeds emerge. The story of Esther unfolds as an allegory of the real tortures besieging domestic workers, as we see a picture of a young woman who lavished care on the family she worked for, only to be taken advantage of and abused. Although Esther tended to Ah Soon like a mother, eventually, as had been foreshadowed, he raped her. Rather than saving her, his parents saw her as dehumanized "evidence" of their son's shame and went on to gruesomely murder their employee by hanging and burning her.

Following this, Ah Soon leapt to his death. But he returned as a spirit in the month of hungry ghosts, and his parents developed a plan to kill Rosa, thereby wedding her to their son in the afterlife. Until now, the Teos did not seem like monsters, but this revelation of their capacity to condone and enact sexual and physical violence and murder supports Tadiar's argument that as "commodities," domestic helpers are seen as expendable.[38] Gender, racial, national, and class difference construct these workers as dehumanized exceptions to universal calls for human rights, and allow people like the Teos, who see themselves as devout and loving, to shed all moral

37 Constable, "Filipina Workers in Hong Kong," 149.
38 Tadiar, *Fantasy Production*, 118.

sensibility. Instead, they objectify their employee and treat her as a thing "manufactured for exploitation."[39]

Having fully transformed their employee into an exploitable commodity, the Teos proceed to tie her up and torture her with burning sticks, as they try to force her to agree to marry Ah Soon in the afterlife. When the torture doesn't work, they attempt to bribe her, promising to bring her younger brother to Singapore and help him to be medically treated by the standards of a wealthy country, pointing to how the violent treatment toward working class characters in the film is a microcosm for the structural violence of a global system that denies proper medical care to large swaths of the world. When Rosa refuses both torture and bribe, her bosses attempt to murder her by hanging, as they did to Esther before her.

The solidarity of hungry ghosts, however, defeats this monstrous plan, as Esther lights Mr. Teo on fire and burns the ropes by which Rosa hangs. As invisible domestic workers, Rosa and Esther become one, and we see that while these workers are abused, they are also incredibly powerful and creative. In the end, it is neither Rosa nor Esther alone who defeat the Teos. In fact, in retrospect, we learn that they were entwined all along. The voiceover that we attributed to Rosa turns out to have been Esther's narration of her own arrival in Singapore. It was easy to confuse one girl's story for the other, since their hopes and dreams as well as their disappointments and terrors were so similar. In the end, their two voices blend as Rosa walks into the airport, headed for the Philippines, carrying Esther's remains. The "monstrous" wraiths haunting Singapore's streets and homes were never the enemy, they were a potential revolutionary army of hungry ghosts who, together, may find a way home.

Reproductive Realism in *Get Out*

The terror of domestic labor is inextricable from the terror of white supremacy. True horror is not a case of "dark" evils against the "light" of virtue. And yet, so often horror films still feature besieged white people in the suburbs cowering against shadowy terrors. In *Get Out*, Jordan Peele's 2017 "social thriller"—a term the director coined to describe horror films in which

---

39 Tadiar, *Fantasy Production*, 118.

oppressive social conditions are found to be the true evil—the racial codes of fear are reversed from the very first scene, in which we are aligned with Andre, a young Black man who becomes lost in a maze-like white suburb. His worst fears come true when he is assaulted and kidnapped by a mysterious stalker. Soon he will be inducted into a form of domestic work akin to slavery.

Unknowingly headed toward this same fate is young Black photographer, Chris Washington, who is preparing to meet the parents of his white girlfriend, Rose Armitage. As the hip couple hang out at Chris's apartment, their easy and humorous rapport establishes them as "post-racial," to the point where Rose can tease Chris for worrying whether her parents know he is not white. But we already see the cracks in this fantasy when the couple set out on a foreboding road trip to the Armitage's house, during which they are confronted by a racist police officer.

Despite Rose's claims that her parents aren't racist, once the couple arrive at their destination Chris must endure the microaggressions commonly perpetrated by liberal people who imagine themselves to be "race blind." Rose's father, Dean, speaks with African American Vernacular English that feels false and condescending. And when Rose's brother, Jeremy, arrives he pays Chris a racist "compliment," observing that his "frame and genetic makeup" could make him a "fucking beast" of an athlete, pointing to "the fetishism and reduction of the Black man to his body," as Jason Read argues.[40] But the creepiest aspect of the household are the domestic workers, Walter and Georgina. Their robotic, stiffly formal appearances are accompanied by bursts of spooky music—the film's formal way of directing our attention to them as the focal point of uncanny terror.

The Armitage family displace their covert racism onto a disgust at Chris's "dirty" addiction to cigarettes. And Rose's psychotherapist mother, Missy, offers to hypnotize him to rid him of the habit. Chris turns her down but she ambushes and hypnotizes him against his will by probing him for the story of his deepest trauma, the night his mother died. When he was a young child, his mother was hit by a car. Waiting for her to return from work, Chris was frozen by fear and denial, and so did nothing but watch TV

---

40 Jason Read, "'You'd be a Beast': *Get Out* and Race," *Unemployed Negativity*, February 27, 2017, http://www.unemployednegativity.com/2017/02/youd-be-beast-get-out-and-race.html.

through the night. Missy expertly exploits Chris's feelings of powerlessness and guilt over this trauma, which allows her to immobilize him, sending his consciousness into "the sunken place"—a dark, endless abyss where he floats and flails, looking up at the world as if through a distant TV screen. Missy presents herself as a maternal, caring figure but she uses psychology to control and degrade Chris, revealing the history of psychiatry as a means to promote scientific racism and other forms of inequality, while also pointing to such medical atrocities as the Tuskegee study, in which Black men were the subjects of experiments and knowingly denied treatment for syphilis.

Chris gradually realizes that it is time to get out of this racist death trap, but by this time it is too late. He is ambushed by the family and awakens shackled in the basement. There he is shown a video that explains the "Coagula" process, in which a white man's consciousness will be transplanted into Chris's body and he will be limited to the role of passenger in his own life, residing in "the sunken place." The Coagula process not only confines people to an endless dark abyss, but it can't be reversed. By the film's end we retroactively understand that the domestic workers in the film, Walter and Georgina, already live in "the sunken place," while their actions are controlled by Dean Armitage's parents. This terror may seem to be the stuff of fantasy, but it corresponds to the real conditions of many domestic workers who must not only work in intimate relation to their employer, but whose labor is dismissed as unimportant and unreal. As Aldon Sajor Marte-Wood explains, "Always on-call and on-demand," the domestic worker lives a half-life, in which their time and body is not their own.[41]

The shadowy existence of the domestic worker is captured by the gothic style of Get Out. As Sarah Ilott argues, the gothic has long been a genre with an ability to "foreground and deconstruct" racism's psychological torment as the "colonization of the mind."[42] In its British mode, this genre conjures castles, aristocracy, and the anxiety of lineage, as well guilt and dark secrets.

41 Alden Sajor Marte-Wood, "Philippine Reproductive Fiction and Crises of Social Reproduction," *Post45: Deindustrialization and the New Cultures of Work,* no. 1 January 10, 2019, https://post45.org/2019/01/philippine-reproductive-fiction-and-crises-of-social-reproduction.

42 Sarah Ilot, "Racism that Grins: African American Gothic Realism and Systemic Critique," *Jordan Peele's* Get Out, edited by Dawn Keetley (Columbus: The Ohio State University Press, 2020), 116.

But the US tradition of gothic is arguably linked most closely to the guilt and trauma of national sins such as the extermination of Native Americans and slavery. In a classic study, Eve Sedgwick argues that the key indicators of the gothic mode are isolation and immobilization, live burial, sleeplike and deathlike states, doubling, and the unspeakable, all of which are central to the horror of *Get Out*.[43] The Coagula process severs a person from her bodily autonomy, relegating her to a sleep-like, zombified state, existing only to channel the will of her master.

Peele's use of gothic conventions to depict the experience of racialized domestic labor corresponds with Theresa Gaddu's notion that gothic tales are not "gateways to other, distant worlds of fantasy" or escapism, but "intimately connected to the culture that produces them."[44] The genre is often trivialized or dismissed as "hackneyed," "feminine," or "popular," but this policing seems to represent a fear of the truth. That is, gothic tales reveal that our national identity is constructed by historical horrors that must be repressed so that we can live with ourselves. *Get Out* draws on this tradition, while making the connection between slavery, domestic labor, and gothic terror explicit. The depiction of zombified black victims, paralyzed and shackled by their "masters," evokes slavery, but also shows that racialized servitude *is still with us*.

The most gothic figures in *Get Out* are Georgina, Walter, and Andre, who have already undergone the Coagula process, and are thus enslaved. It is no accident that they are all domestic workers. Georgina is the Armitage's maid, Walter is their groundskeeper, and Andre is a sex slave and domestic servant to a much older woman. These characters' gothic status is confirmed in their every gesture and in every shot that frames them. Their anachronistic diction, their mannered acting style, and the zooms, jump-cuts, and musical cues that accompany their appearances all point to their disconnection from realism and their submersion in gothic horror "irrealism," a term Michael Löwy uses to describe fiction that produces a conceptual

43 Eve Kosofsky Sedgwick, *The Coherence of Gothic Conventions* (London: Routledge, 1986).
44 Teresa A. Goddu, *Gothic America: Narrative, History and Nation* (New York: Columbia University Press, 1997), 2.

truth of history rather than a literal replica of events.[45] The irrealism of the film's domestic servants is highlighted by their contrast to the Armitages and Chris himself, who, not having undergone the Coagula process, speaks in naturalistic modern diction and is shot in a traditionally realistic style.

Adding to their uncanniness, all three domestic servants are clearly compared to the robots in *The Stepford Wives* in moments where they "glitch." In the original film, white housewives are transformed into perfected robots who live only to perform reproductive labor. There are moments, however, where these robots glitch out—crashing their cars, spilling their drinks at parties, devolving into repetitive movements and speech patterns. These malfunctions expose "women's work" as unnatural by contributing to what Marina Vishmidt calls "reproductive realism," formal approaches that refuse to decontextualize reproduction from "gendered and racialised and colonial specificity."

These works find innovative formal techniques that avoid an "affirmative politics." Vishmidt implies that affirmation would simply confer a "positive" rather than "negative" identity on those who do feminized labor, such as the figure of the compassionate housekeeper in the film *Roma*. Instead of championing and elevating individual maids and housewives, these artworks force us to contend with flaws in an economic system that subordinates and devalues feminized people and their activities.[46] The glitching in *The Stepford Wives* is one of these formal devices of "reproductive realism" in that the gesture does not reveal positive qualities in the character. Instead, it shows how her behavior is forced and unnatural.

In an early scene of *Get Out*, Georgina glitches in a similar way to the Stepford wives, distractedly pouring iced tea into Chris's glass until it overflows. As she does this, the sound of the Armitage family's banal chat fades out and is encompassed by swelling eerie music. Abruptly she shifts back into her robotic character, a strangely stiff figure who talks, moves, and dresses anachronistically all while wearing a strained, non-naturalistic smile, a picture of both victim and perpetrator of what Ilott calls "racism

---

45 Michael Löwy, "The Current of Critical Irrealism: 'A moonlit enchanted night,'" in Matthew Beaumont, ed., *A Concise Companion to Realism* (Hoboken: Wiley-Blackwell, 2010).
46 Marina Vishmidt. "Reproductive Realism: Towards a Critical Aesthetics of Gendered Labor," Histórias Feministas seminar, 2018, Museu de Arte São Paulo.

that grins." This acting style, in which exaggerated expressions are abruptly assumed and discarded, is another aspect of "reproductive realism," highlighting the artificiality of behavior, and pointing to the ways domestic workers are coerced into the expression of emotions that are not their own.

The most masterful moment of this acting style occurs during a conversation between Chris and Georgina. She is apologizing to Chris for disconnecting his phone, holding herself rigidly and using the uncanny old-fashioned diction of the matriarch that so jarringly contrasts with Chris's hip vernacular. He uses casual language in an attempt to bond with the Black domestic workers employed by the Armitages, and every time this fails to connect, Chris experiences a surge of fear. For Chris, the domestic workers who look so comforting and act so strangely embody the uncanny.

Another way Chris tries to forge connections with the few other Black people on the estate is to frankly confess his discomfort at being surrounded by white people. This empathetic confession breaks Georgina's façade and the woman inside briefly surfaces, as she shares Chris's experience of marginalization and suffering at the hands of the whites. In a magisterial performance, actor Betty Gabriel's face goes to war with itself as her tears and pain struggle against her keeper's bland, cold discipline and fake concern. The matriarch wins out but she still glitches as she repeats the word "no" over and over, trying to get the cadence right, until she resolves fully into the matriarch's personality.

This is shown as a tight close-up, allowing Georgina's synthetic recalibrations of "warmth" to be registered in excruciating detail. She fully dispossesses the woman whom she occupies with the assertion, "The Armitages are so good to us. They treat us like family," revealing the violence at the heart of the "familial" status accorded to domestic workers.

In this scene and others, domestic labor is depicted as a series of rigid acting gestures that are sometimes cut through with pathos and other times interrupted by glitches. These gestures denaturalize what Arlie Hochschild calls the "deep acting" required of those employed in feminized service jobs, who find their true feelings drowned out by the compelled performances of emotional labor they must enact. This can also be connected to what the Marxist playwright Bertolt Brecht called an "alienation effect," a style of acting that estranges us from our expectations of human behavior and shows that our emotions are constructed by larger social forces.

In other scenes, the classic gothic trope of uncanny doubling is brought into play to depict Georgina's deep dispossession. After his first uncomfortable day with the Armitages, Chris goes out for an evening smoke. Through the window he sees Georgina standing zombie-like, seeming to stare straight ahead. Slowly and deliberately, she fixes her hair. As we cut to a shot from inside her room, we see her uncannily self-absorbed expression and it becomes evident that she is using the window as a mirror. As we learn later, her gaze is multiple; she is both the Armitage matriarch and the unnamed woman whose body was snatched to accommodate her. This double gaze is thematized by the reflecting surfaces that surround her.

The reflection and refraction of gazes is repeated shortly before Chris's body is auctioned off, as he wanders around the Armitage's garden, taking pictures. Through his lens he spots Georgina at the same window. This time her back is to him and she faces a mirror. Through the mirror she spots him and abruptly turns, uncannily meeting the gaze of his lens. He sheepishly turns away. Her jolting motions and multiple reflections and gazes estrange us from a single understanding of her as a domestic worker, and ensure that her labor is deconstructed and denaturalized, contributing to a "reproductive realism."

The depiction of Georgina as a fractured and multiple being supports Evelyn Nakano Glenn's assertion that in order to comprehend how reproductive labor works we must move away from an "additive model" of understanding multiple oppressions. Instead, she asserts, we should develop an integrated model that sees oppressions as interlocking. She points to the historical division of reproductive labor. As white women were convinced that they should develop themselves mentally and spiritually to become the "soul" of the domestic hearth, women of color were enlisted to take on the "dirty" chores that provided for its physical maintenance.[47] This division of labor needed to be maintained by "proving" women of color deserved to be relegated to these lower-order tasks and this was done by humiliating and degrading them. Nakano Glenn describes this relationship between white

---

47 Nakano Glenn, "From Servitude to Service Work," 8.

women and women of color as one of *"interdependence,"* as their self-definitions are inseparable from these hierarchies. Georgina embodies this interlocking and interdependent relationship, as two women who are in a contest for power and existence war within her.

Part of this interdependence in the division of reproductive labor was the idea that women of color were destined to care for white children while neglecting their own families. This is underscored by Chris's backstory. While Missy preys on Chris's vulnerability—his sense of responsibility for his mother's death—the real trauma is social. When he was only a small child his mother's job forced her to leave him alone. Like many Black women, she was not given the privilege of reproducing her own family; she had to go out—perhaps to care for someone else's family—while her son stayed home, without any childcare. Her death, the original source of Chris's trauma, conveys the wrenching separation of Black families in the service of white, middle-class life.

Get Out is a social thriller that demonstrates the impossibility of separating public and private terror; the economic is shot through with gendered and racialized violence, and the home is no shelter from the crudest forces of capitalism. In a moment where racialized, feminized labor is naturalized and undervalued, *Get Out* points to the profound horror that this erasure and violence brings. And yet, the film does not end in victimization. Instead, the "racial paranoia" that the horror genre exposes is what helps characters survive, as Dawn Keetley argues.[48] Not only does Chris escape becoming a slave in the Armitage household, but Walter, another domestic worker whose body has been snatched by the family's patriarch, is able to resurface for long enough to fatally wound Rose and kill himself, and in doing so killing another member of the family. The film does not only illuminate the mythologies of "natural" domestic labor but insists that these conditions are riddled with contradictions and openings for retributive violence, a way to "get out."

48 Dawn Keetley, "Introduction," in Dawn Keetley, ed., *Jordan Peele's* Get Out (Columbus: The Ohio State University Press, 2020), 4.

Haunted Domesticity in *La Llorona*

In 1982 and 1983 the tyrannical regime of Guatemalan dictator José Efraín Ríos Montt escalated a war against leftist guerillas fighting for land reform and democratization. Not only were these fighters massacred, but "*la violencia*" was extended to anyone who appeared to support or abet them. These "scorched-earth campaigns" disproportionately affected Indigenous Mayan's. Over 100,000 deaths and 40,000 disappearances were officially recorded. Between 80,000 and 250,000 orphans were left behind.[49]

When director Jayro Bustamante set out to make a film that explored the aftermath of these horrors, he faced many challenges. Not only did Guatemala lack a national cinema, but many in the country's middle class didn't want to discuss this topic, let alone watch a film about it. However, he realized, what they *did* want to watch was horror films. This genre, he decided, was the best way to break the silence. To further drive the urgency of this topic home, he placed his ghost story in a domestic setting, a haunted house that would serve as a "microcosm for the sins of the Guatemalan government and the tension between its complacent, bourgeois parties and the native people they either destroyed or ignored."[50]

Bustamante merged the haunted house story with a popular Latin American folktale, the story of La Llorona. Before Spanish colonization this figure was a protective deity, but her story was hijacked by colonizing narratives, and she became known as a "monstrous woman" who had drowned her own children to avenge herself on her departed lover. In *La Llorona* Bustamante reclaims this myth, changing the titular figure from a misogynist caricature (as she was portrayed in the film simultaneously made in the US, *The Curse of La Llorona*), to a figure of righteous vengeance against the Ríos Montt regime—as Bustamante puts it, "she is a princess looking for justice. She is not crying for men; she is crying for more relevant things like the suffering of her people."[51]

49 Emily Rosser, "Depoliticised Speech and Sexed Visibility: Women, Gender and Sexual Violence in the 1999 Guatemalan *Comisión para el Esclarecimiento Histórico* Report," *The International Journal of Transitional Justice* 1, no. 3 (December 2007): 392.

50 Ryan Lattanzio, "Jayro Bustamante Is Building the Guatemalan Film Industry from Scratch with Movies Like 'La Llorona,'" *IndieWire*, March 21, 2021, https://www.indiewire.com/2021/03 la-llorona-jayro-bustamante-guatemalan-oscar-contender-1234621408/.

51 Lattanzio, "Jayro Bustamante is Building."

The film begins in the home of General Enrique Monteverde, a thinly disguised version of Ríos Montt. His wife and the wives of other war criminals are praying to their Christian god to protect their husbands from prosecution during upcoming human rights trials. That night, as the General lies awake in bed, he hears mysterious weeping. When he goes to find the source, he is startled by a sudden sound and shoots off his gun, nearly killing his wife, Carmen.

As the family cluster around the General, the servants speak to each other in Kaqchikel, a Mayan Indigenous language, affirming that the Monteverde's house is haunted and that they must leave. When they announce their resignation to the family, they are met with hostile reproach. Calling themselves "generous employers," the family hurl insults at their employees, chastising them for their lack of gratitude. Even Natalia, the General's daughter, who perceives herself as more enlightened than her explicitly racist, classist parents, defends her family's paternalism: "My parents have been good to you. They treat you like family. They buy you tortillas. No one else is going to treat you like they do," she says. Despite this attempt to cow them, the domestic workers remain composed and demand their benefits. Finally, they are dismissed with Carmen's warning: "no one will ever hire you."

The trial against the General begins with moving testimony given by an Indigenous woman wearing an elaborate veil. With a faint voice, almost extinguished by grief, but without embarrassment, she tells, through a Spanish translator, the story of her community, of having their crops, homes, and clothes set on fire, of being raped and seeing their husbands murdered, of fleeing, starving, and being taken to a military base where women were yet again raped. This testimony echoes the story of thousands of people during this genocidal period of Guatemala's history. During the trial, the General's defense lawyer claims that all these victims were "insurgents," but the film makes it clear that Ríos Montt's was a ruthless campaign in which large swaths of Indigenous people were raped, made destitute, and massacred, regardless of their participation in the fighting.

At the end of the trial, the judge finds the General guilty and the people explode in joy, but he is never punished for his crime. His wife, who has prayed for his exoneration, is deeply complicitous in a logic that dehumanizes the women who were raped and tortured, calling them prostitutes and insinuating that the officers magnanimously offered them positions as maids, which the women were too lazy to take. At this point, Carmen is committed to rendering Indigenous women as "monsters," akin to the caricature of La Llorona. This labeling allows infinite cruelty while elevating her war criminal husband. As Jeffrey Jerome Cohen argues in his famous manifesto on monsters, "representing an anterior culture as monstrous justifies its displacement by rendering the act heroic."[52]

When the people realize that the Guatemalan government's widespread corruption will allow the General to remain free, thousands of protestors surround his house, holding up pictures of the loved ones they lost to his tyrannical dictatorship. They remain day and night, demanding justice. Out of the masses, Alma emerges to replace the domestic servants who have fled. She appears as a solemn figure, dressed in white, first seen as part of the crowd, but materializing as a silent haunting force that does not so much leave the furious crowd behind, but concentrates and radiates their anger.

In his creation of Alma as La Llorona, Bustamante reimagines and radically revises the familiar elements of the traditional myth. The story of La Llorona has been told and retold for centuries but the basic elements of the tale are that a woman of low social stature, often imagined as Indigenous, is seduced by a conquistador or otherwise privileged man. They fall in love and have two children together but eventually he abandons her, often leaving her for a woman of his own class. In a vengeful fury, La Llorona drowns the children she shares with him and is immediately consumed by regret. She is forever after doomed to haunt the body of water where she drowned her children, crying and calling out for them. Often pictured as a spooky figure in a long white gown, she is commonly seen as a threat, who will steal other people's children to replace her own.

The tale, in its primal elements, is easily interpreted misogynistically. In many aspects La Llorona is the definition of what Barbara Creed has defined as the "monstrous feminine," a common horror-film villain that

---

52 Jeffrey Jerome Cohen, "'Monster Culture' (Seven Theses)," in *The Monster Theory Reader*, ed. Jeffrey Andrew Weinstock (University of Minnesota Press, 2020), 41.

represents the stigmatization of women and their bodily functions. As a murderous mother who "leaks" tears she embodies what Creed sees as a patriarchal disgust with qualities that are seen as "feminine," such as irrationality, emotionality, and indeterminacy as well as bodily excesses related to menstruation, sexuality, and pregnancy. It is this process of "othering" the feminine and making it monstrous that creates and sustains dominant identity, Cohen argues, "imbu[ling] meaning to the Us and Them behind every cultural mode of seeing."[53]

Even if she elicits some sympathy, in murdering her children La Llorona is condemned to this exterior space, beyond the pale of the thinkable. This makes the myth open to readings that Domino Renee Perez argues "reinforce conventional ideas about sex, morality, gender roles, and sexuality."[54] However, these tropes are critically interrogated in such revisions as the literary works of Pat Mora, Gloria Anzaldua, Cherrie Moraga, Sandra Cisneros, and Alma Luz Villanueva, the Hernandez Brothers' comic *Love and Rockets*, the artwork of Lizz Lopez, Carlos Encinas, and David Salas, and activist performances such as the 2017 "Procesión de las 43 Lloronas." The lore becomes here a "site of resistance to dominative or other oppressive practices," Perez argues.[55] Miriam L. Fernandez looks at the revision of history in these retellings as "rhetorical hauntings" or "memories as acts of resistance."[56] The Llorona story is so common and ritualistic across Latinx cultures that it becomes infinitely "adaptable to new contexts because the repertoire both keeps and transforms choreographies of meaning," Fernandez argues.[57]

Bustamante's retelling is in the spirit of the protest that motivated "Procesión de las 43 Lloronas," an action to commemorate and demand that the Mexican government take responsibility for the forty-three student teachers who were abducted and disappeared from Ayotzinapa Guerrero in 2014. In the film La Llorona is converted from a threat to a

---

53 Cohen, "Monster Culture," 51.

54 Domino Renee Perez, *There Was a Woman: La Llorona from Folklore to Popular Culture* (University of Texas Press, 2008), 22.

55 Perez, *There Was a Woman*, 69.

56 Miriam L. Fernandez, "La Llorona and Rhetorical Haunting in Mexico's Public Sphere," *Journal for the History of Rhetoric* 24, no. 1 (2021): 55.

57 Fernandez, "La Llorona and Rhetorical Haunting," 57.

protective spirit. Her children die, but it is the murderous General who is responsible. She tells her story by seeping into his wife's dreams, where we learn that during *"la violencia,"* Alma was a poor Indigenous villager. Monteverde's soldiers invaded her small mountain town and interrogated her, assuming her husband was a guerilla fighter. When she had no information to give, they forced her to watch them drown her children before killing her.

Before we are privy to her supernatural status as La Llorona, we already begin to see Alma as a symbol of the continuity between domestic labor and colonial brutality. Alison Crosby, who interviewed and researched female victims of the Ríos Montt regime, notes that these women's traumas did not end after the rapes and murders they experienced or witnessed. Rather, for them, violence against women is experienced as "a heavy load" in the present, as they suffer the lasting effects of having their land and loved ones stolen. The experience of working as poor peasants and domestic servants is defined by the same logic of gendered, racialized warfare in which Indigenous people were viewed as culturally inferior, incapable of real feeling, and sexually available.[58]

When women survivors were given space to speak and process the long-term impacts of the war, they emphasized that physical violence can't be separated from economic violence, or from difficult, but ordinary, "woman's work." Because of this, Crosby argues that it is necessary to connect the war crimes of the past to the reproduction of daily life in the present. Truth and reconciliation commissions may miss this, becoming "a story about racism or about specific, individual rights violations rather than about long-term, systemic abuse born of a colonial project with economic objectives."[59] The reality for Indigenous people is that the sins of the war extend both backward to the origins of colonial dispossession and forward to contemporary gendered, racialized, oppressive conditions of domestic labor.

The degraded status of women's work in the present is inextricable from this historical violence and colonialism toward Indigenous women. As Elsa M. Chaney and Mary Garcia Castro argue, in Latin America (as

---

58 Alison Crosby, "Carrying a Heavy Load: Mayan Women's Understandings of Reparation in the Aftermath of Genocide," *Journal of Genocide Research* 18, no. 2–3, (2016), 273.

59 Crosby, "Carrying a Heavy Load," 276.

elsewhere) domestic work is devalued as are the people who are forced to perform this work. Rather than being a legitimate occupation, it is relegated to "women's work," something that women who are "invisible to themselves and to society" are born to do.[60] This legacy of degradation often means that these jobs are not legally classified or protected as work while entailing low wages, intense isolation, long hours, little mobility, and frequent abuse. Theoretically, these conditions could lead to solidarity between Indigenous domestic workers and middle-class women who must also grapple with patriarchal structures. But, as we see in *La Llorona*, bourgeois women are compromised, often relying on domestic workers in their own households. As in the case of Carmen, for many elite women the domestic worker is the key to "maintain[ing] their privileged status in capitalist society," as Keri Anne Brondo argues.[61] Rather than challenging patriarchy within the family, these women may reinforce it, gaining their freedom through displacing the household gender imbalance onto domestic workers.

One night Alma is sexually harassed by the General, who follows her into her bathroom. Rather than protect Alma from her husband, Carmen scolds her for wearing her uniform too tightly. This experience of sexual harassment is compounded by the fact that we know Alma must also be subject to the same degradation we witnessed earlier, as the previous servants were offered tortillas rather than benefits and threatened with destitution for daring to insist on their rights. Like the servants before her, Alma stands up for herself. But because of her supernatural powers she can do more than refuse, she can destroy. As Fernandez says of La Llorona's activist revisions, "the haunted can become the haunters when they transmit memories of collective trauma and pain onto the public sphere in a quest for change and justice."[62]

The middle-class women in the Monteverde household do not want to recognize the rising tide of the oppressed seeping through their

---

60 Elsa M. Chaney and Mary Garcia Castro, "Introduction," in Chaney and Castro, ed. *Muchachas No More: Household Workers in Latin America and the Caribbean* (Philadelphia: Temple University Press, 1989), 3–4.

61 Keri Anne Brondo, *A Maid's Worldview: Assessing Aspirations in Guatemala City's Domestic Sector*, Dissertation, Iowa State University, 1999, 23.

62 Fernandez, "La Llorona and Rhetorical Haunting," 56.

house in flooded bathrooms and swimming pools. But soon they can't look away from the reflective pools that mirror back their own complicity in a vast system of racialized, gendered, colonial violence. La Llorona forces the truth onto Carmen, infiltrating her dreams and compelling this apologist for genocide to live out Alma's terrors night after night. As Carmen witnesses her husband's brutal actions firsthand, she must finally understand that her own privilege has been based on the bloodshed of hundreds of thousands of innocent Indigenous people like Alma and her children.[63] Now Carmen must recognize both the connection and disconnection she has to Alma, and her own responsibility to right the wrongs of her class. In response she kills her husband as the other women in her family look on, hinting that real solidarity of white middle class women with Indigenous domestic workers can't be piecemeal. The film, rather, is a call, as Sophie Lewis puts it, "to turn race traitor and decolonial accomplice."[64]

This final solidarity between Alma and Carmen is not based on similarity, but rather, as Evelyn Nakano Glenn reminds us, on a critical understanding of *interdependence*. These women are tied together through structural hierarchies and chains of complicity as well as common causes. As La Llorona, Alma seems to recognize this complexity, choosing to spare Carmen, who has been indirectly responsible for her suffering. Like the water that infuses Carmen's house and undoes its orderly cruelty, Alma chooses to seep into Carmen's consciousness, forcing her enemy to understand her own role in these hierarchies and, by doing so, forging a path to undoing them.

Conclusion: Ambivalent Solidarity as Werewolf Lovechild

In the Brazilian horror fantasy *Good Manners*, a white, middle-class woman and her Black maid fall in love, but this does not inoculate them from the disease of hierarchal power dynamics. Clara shows up for an interview with

---

63 Joanna Page and Ignacio M. Sánchez Prado, "Temporalities in Latin American Film," *Arizona Journal of Hispanic Cultural Studies* 16 (2012): 203–10.

64 Sophie Lewis, "She Wants Your Children," *Blind Field Journal*, May 18, 2021, https://blindfieldjournal.com/2021/05/18/she-wants-your-children.

Ana, a heavily pregnant white woman who is living alone in a posh section of São Paulo. The job was advertised as a nanny position but during the interview Clara learns that she will also be cleaning and cooking. Although more qualified people have applied for the job, Ana hires Clara because she is easy to manipulate. Clara lacks references and is clearly desperate for money. It goes unsaid, but the fact that she is Black also makes her more vulnerable to abuse. Immediately after hiring Clara, Ana acts exploitatively and inappropriately, insisting that Clara be on-call constantly and drunkenly sitting on her lap. One full-moon night when Clara returns from a brief outing she finds Ana sleepwalking and foraging in the refrigerator. When she tries to lead Ana back to bed, Ana kisses her passionately. Clara reciprocates, but Ana bites her neck, making her bleed.

Still, the women become lovers and Clara turns into Ana's protector. When, on another full moon night, Ana kills and eats a cat as she sleepwalks, Clara doesn't run. Instead, she supports her boss's monstrous development, cutting her own hand to add blood to Ana's meals. One night, as Clara is out on an errand, Ana is pierced by intense pain. She lays down and her rippling belly bursts. Clara returns to find her eviscerated boss/lover breathing her last. In a sorrowful haze, she turns to shoot the beast that had erupted from Ana, but when she spots the helpless infant werewolf, she can't bring herself to kill it. Instead, she adopts the werewolf child and spends the rest of the film sacrificing herself to raise and protect him.

As the housekeeper and caretaker for Ana, Clara is not simply a victim. Their tender and gorgeous love and sex scenes are genuinely transgressive, making it impossible to deny their status as lesbian outlaws. And there is some solidarity between them as well. As an unwed pregnant person, Ana suffers under the same patriarchal system that has kept Clara impoverished and precarious. And yet, Ana also contributes to this system. She exploits Clara's racialized, feminized precarity to maintain her swank lifestyle and to surround herself with love and care, even as her middle-class world rejects her. My guess is that, had she lived, when Ana regained entry into her own social stratum, Clara would have been left by the wayside.

The monstrosity of this condition is that Clara experiences this exploitation as *love* and so, even after Ana's death, she can't free herself from it. Joel, Ana's werewolf son, is both a beautiful, sweet boy and a murderous monster. As an extension of Ana's bourgeois, white privilege, he continues to dominate Clara's life, keeping her from stability and egalitarian love. But as a monster he is also truly Clara and Ana's love child, a figure of outlaw solidarity. Clara's love for him is a confusing mix of servitude and feral identification.

Good Manners shows the relationship between white, middle-class housewives and racialized, low-waged domestic workers to be a slippery slope of solidarity and antagonism. Both exist as figures whose work is disguised as *nature*. Both have grievances that are dismissed or repressed by the ideology that all love and care are willingly given as gifts and are undeserving of compensation. And yet, the white housewife benefits from the hyperexploitation and invisibility of her employee. Instead of fighting against patriarchal forms, the "mistress of the house" displaces her anger, heaping the work she doesn't want to do on her vulnerable subordinate. Explaining this relationship means we have to rid ourselves of simplifications and "additive" explanations of oppression. Instead we must grapple with interlocking oppressions and complicated, structural truths. Only then can Clara and Ana's werewolf love child howl at the moon and truly run free.

CHAPTER 3

THE TELLTALE MANAGED HEART: SERVICE LABOR AND EMOTIONAL LABOR IN CONTEMPORARY HORROR

When the subject of crazy jobs comes up, I often bring up Laura Y, for whom I briefly worked as a personal assistant. When I arrived at her home for the job interview, I was told by another personal assistant that she had environmental allergies and that I would need to change into a hypoallergenic garment she provided. I was led into a small shed where I was given a scentless but severely stained white sheet with a hole through which to poke my head. Shed of the professional work clothes I had worn to the interview, I was escorted to Ms. Y's gothic, crepuscular dining room. With a startling creak, I sank deep into a tentacular armchair, draped in lace webbing, and was handed a faintly medicinal smelling glass of tea. In the shadows, I could detect the mouse-like movements of other assistants. I felt the chill of a wind on my naked legs and shivered a little at the approach of Ms. Y's gaunt, translucent form.

Every instinct told me to flee, but a quick review of my life up until this moment stopped me in my tracks. I was a child of parents who woke up early from the American Dream, with a start. Before I was eighteen my parents suffered the slings and arrows of this country's toxic family values, precarious job market, cruel individualism, and bad healthcare. My dad lost his middle-class job, my parents divorced, the family suffered generalized depression and dysfunction, and finally, after faulty treatment at Kaiser hospital, my dad died of cancer before he was fifty.

Jobs had never been optional. I started at age thirteen, working at Kentucky Fried Chicken, sinking below the counter when I saw my junior high school peers walk in the door. Following this came a series of gigs as a filing clerk, recycler, children's party planner, copy machine operator, substitute elementary school teacher, flyer distributor, porn film processor, political fundraiser, house cleaner, SAT prepper, freelance tutor (of pretty much everything, I just faked it), and whatever else I could get. (One of the weirdest was an elocution teacher—don't ask.) I was like the picaresque "zany" described by Sianne Ngai in her discussion of precarity and emotional labor: "the needy man doesn't walk like the rest, he skips, twists, cringes, crawls. He spends his life choosing and performing positions."[1]

And still, I was always just getting by, living in food deserts, scraping up rent for studio apartments with faulty plumbing, subsisting on table scraps and $1 slices of pizza. I arrived in Oakland licking my wounds as I fled from a graduate program I couldn't afford to complete. But I didn't return alone, I was accompanied by tens of thousands of dollars in student loans (they still live with me today!) As in the escalating terrors of a horror movie, my life had reached the point where there was no way out. I was trapped in whatever job would take me.

So I went with the flow, responded to both work-related and personal questions, modulated my tone to confidentiality when Ms. Y wanted to discuss the various friends and ex-employees who had slighted and disappointed her. I was rewarded with a low-paying job that entailed recording and transcribing her every random word and thought (to what end I never learned). But more than that, to smile, to agree, to placate.

Like most people socialized as women, I'm not sure how I learned to master the performance of these ineffable qualities—pliancy, agreeableness, flexibility, gentle indulgence—but they have served me well in getting many jobs, although most of them were low-paid and insecure. I am in some measure proud of my capabilities but part of me mourns the loss of my "real" emotions under these conditions. As in a horror movie, my "feelings," whatever they may be, call faintly to me from beyond, through the walls that have

---

1 Sianne Ngai, *Our Aesthetic Categories* (Cambridge: Harvard University Press, 2015), 191.

protected me from hunger and homelessness. As in Edgar Allen Poe's classic horror story, "The Telltale Heart," the muted throbs of these supposedly dead and buried emotions will never entirely fade away.

In her still relevant 1983 book *The Managed Heart: Commercialization of Human Feeling*, Arlie Hochschild studies stewardesses to try to understand the impacts of emotional labor, such as serving customers with a smile, absorbing unwanted flirtation, and deflecting insults and ill-treatment. She argues that the explosion of service jobs for companies that are selling ephemeral qualities, such as happiness or calm, has a deep impact on the psyches of employees, "estrang[ing] workers from their own smiles."[2] This is another way that capitalist logic is extending into the far reaches of daily life. Once a worker has internalized their "Delta smile," they can't just turn it off at night: "Seeming to 'love the job' becomes part of the job," and it is easier to seem to love the job if you just make yourself believe that you do.[3] Love becomes a job that can't be left at the workplace.

This compulsion to care goes beyond performing emotions for others, we must also learn to love our jobs themselves. As Kathi Weeks argues, the charged romantic energy that people were once compelled to pour into marriage is now often redirected towards work.[4] A whole host of TED Talks, management texts, and self-help books insist that happiness and productivity at work requires a relentless, enthusiastic love of our jobs. What Betty Friedan called the "feminine mystique" has morphed into the "career mystique," a romantic intensity towards work. In undergoing this emotional discipline, all workers are feminized, since it is women who have been deeply conditioned to "live for love." No matter how we define our gender, in our marriage or to our jobs we are the devoted wives while work takes on the position of the demanding husband.

Horror helps us raise the question, as many feminists have—what would happen if we went on a smile strike? How would things change if

---

2 Arlie Hochschild, *The Managed Heart: Commercialization of Human Feeling* (Berkeley: University of California Press, 2003), 4.

3 Hochschild, *The Managed Heart*, 6.

4 Kathi Weeks, "Down with Love: Feminist Critique and the New Ideologies of Work," *Verso Blog*, Feb 13, 2018, https://www.versobooks.com. blogs/3614-down-with-love-feminist-critique-and-the-new-ideologies-of-work.

we refused emotional work? In her work on feminist approaches to "killing joy," Sarah Ahmed argues that we have been duped by a society that forces us to act as if we *are* happy, when really, we are being forced to *appear* cheerful to comfort those privileged enough to define happiness according to their own needs. If, for instance, we claim that the work of housewives generally makes them happy, then exploitative husbands can argue that their partners do not experience housework as a duty or burden, instead it is an enjoyable *labor of love*. So, the housewife's "happiness" simply smooths over any qualms the husband might feel in taking advantage of her free labor.

In response, Ahmed argues that feminists should reclaim unhappiness, not because we are "against happiness," who could be? But because unhappiness can be a form of rebellion against a definition of happiness that goes against our own true potential for joy. The feminist who cannot help but feel rage, then, is an "affect alien, estranged by happiness."[5] She is from another world, mystified by the forced smiles she sees around her. And yet, this unhappiness can lead to solidarity. As in the horror film *They Live*, which exposes a world dominated by predatory aliens blending invisibly into society, together as feminists we can put on magic sunglasses allowing us to see the truth of our conditions, and bond together to fight back. "There can be joy in killing joy," says Ahmed.[6]

Killing joy puts a wrench in what Patricia Clough has called our contemporary "affect economy," in which "value is sought in the expansion or contraction of affective capacity."[7] Affect—or the performance of emotion, personality, feeling, mood, and care—has come to be seen as a natural resource akin to coal or water, but one that is limitless. Whether it is flirting with a customer or "liking" a Facebook post, affect feeds the maw of capitalism by making sure that emotion and care are constantly contributing to economic expansion.

The rise of affective labor has been key to capitalist transformations since the 1970s, but we see few new realist film traditions that capture the

---

5 Sara Ahmed, "Killing Joy: Feminism and the History of Happiness," *Signs: Journal of Women in Culture and Society* 35, no. 3 (Spring 2010): 581.

6 Ahmed, "Killing Joy," 592.

7 Patricia Ticineto Clough and Jean Halley, eds., *The Affective Turn: Theorizing the Social* (Durham: Duke University Press, 2007), 25.

impacts on these workers.[8] Films of the last fifty years that depict service workers and emotional labor tend to "humanize" the relation of service workers to their employers and customers, while describing how heroically these workers achieve "balance" between their own needs and the demands of their jobs. Or worse, these films fantasize that performing emotions are key to a Cinderella-like transformation for the worker, as in the classic work of ideology *Pretty Woman* (1990) which imagines a prostitute's interaction with a customer magically transforming into "real love," rather than acknowledging that the performance of love is hard work for most sex workers.

Horror films, on the other hand, can depict service work and emotional labor in their full panoply of terrors, portraying workers divested of their futures, personalities, and even their lives. In this chapter you will encounter an "antisocial" network of monsters who refuse to play the game, thereby exposing emotional labor for what it is, a horror show.

Serve or Die: *Maps to the Stars*

Maps to the Stars explores the horror of one of the most intimate positions on offer in the service economy, the role of the personal assistant. This position is perhaps the most exemplary case of emotional labor, as the worker is generally "on the job" 24/7 and their duties are typically nebulous. This job is also a key example of the ways that emotional labor which women performed for free in the home is now manipulated and transformed to fit the demands of waged labor. In this work, there is no possibility for autonomy or distance—the secret truth at the heart of this type of employment is that the worker has been hired to blur the lines between servant and friend.

In *Maps to the Stars*, we witness the trials of a personal assistant blown up to the scale of Greek tragedy. In this modern myth, a disfigured, abused young woman is hired as a personal assistant, or what her boss calls a "chore whore," and the emotional labor extracted from her drives her over the brink

---

8   There are notable exceptions, such as the films Lauren Berlant discusses as the French "cinema of precarity" in their book *Cruel Optimism* or the US films *American Honey, The Florida Project, Support the Girls*, and *Tangerine*. Like horror films, these naturalistic films reject the individualizing psychology and narrative closure that characterize the bulk of Hollywood "realist" films.

of madness. The film begins as a young woman, Agatha, gets off a bus that took her from Florida to Los Angeles. She hires a limousine to meet her and takes a tour around Hollywood, seeking information about celebrities. She is especially interested in the former home of child star, Benjie Weiss, who is known for a movie franchise called *Bad Babysitter*. By referencing both the performance and refusal of childcare, the title of this film already points to emotional labor and its refusal.

We then meet an array of characters whose work as emotional laborers has distorted their personalities to the point of monstrosity. There is Benjie, whose wild popularity as a child star has made him insufferable and cruel. He hurls antisemitic insults at his manager, trivializes his visit to a dying girl in the hospital, and is already a jaded, ex-drug addict at the age of thirteen. He shares an agent with Havana Segrand, a terribly spoiled and damaged actress who is perpetually seeking attention and throwing tantrums. We are introduced to her as she receives a massage and new-age pep talk from Benjie's father, Stafford Weiss, a callow self-help guru who performs deep empathy for a living but really cares only for his own gain.

Stafford Weiss, it turns out, is Agatha's estranged father, who has banished Agatha from the family, after she had a psychotic break. While he coaches workers and families to perform happiness and care, he instrumentalizes his own family, who are all on the precipice of suicidal despair. Despite his fame as a healer, he refuses to acknowledge their pain. Instead of empathy he offers what Jules Evans calls "TED-esque optimism," where happiness is mandatory and positive thinking rules the political and social landscape.[9] As Barbara Ehrenreich claims, "positivity is not so much our condition or our mood as it is part of our ideology—the way we explain the world and think we ought to function within it."[10]

Under this enforced regime of happiness, those who suffer from insecure circumstances are told to see their condition as an opportunity to be embraced as well as a personal responsibility. Even the burn scars that cover Agatha's body should be seen as a "gift" in this "bright sided" culture. The

---

9 Jules Evans, "Solving Happiness," *The New Inquiry*, June 6, 2012, https://thenewinquiry. com/solving-happiness/.

10 Barbara Ehrenreich, *Bright Sided: How the Relentless Promotion of Positive Thinking Has Undermined America* (New York: Metropolitan Books, 2009), 4.

fallout from a world guided by a "happiness industry" of self-help jargon is that it "ends up blaming and medicating individuals for their own misery and ignores the context that has contributed to it."[11] The therapeutic ethos that pervades our culture is presented to us as a means for self-expression. But instead, as Eva Illouz argues, it "extends the credo of the Protestant ethic by making one responsible even for one's emotional destiny."[12]

With this logic, people are responsible for their own suffering, and the social forces that structure their oppression remain invisible. Empathy is seen as a form of enabling pessimistic behavior. According to this anti-empathetic stance, "negative people," meaning anyone who it is not convenient to deal with, deserve to be distanced or abolished from one's life, as was seen in a horrific *New York Times* article advising that we use the pandemic as a way to reorganize our social lives. According to the article's author, Kate Murphy, we should take the opportunity to "cull" and "curate" our friend group, ridding ourselves of burdensome depressed and over-weight friends who may drag us down with them.[13]

This logic that demands compliant happiness "or else" rules the decisions made by the Weiss family, who permanently ostracize Agatha and are immune to her pleas for help and forgiveness. When he finds out she has returned to L.A., Stafford menacingly invades her hotel room, insisting that she leave town. Agatha responds that she is "in recovery" and has returned to "make amends," but even though she is using language from the books that he wrote, Stafford sneers at her use of self-help rhetoric, as it is not suited to his own individualistic purposes. When she asks why he never came to see her at the institution where she was confined, he responds with callous dismissal—"that's a victim question … that's an I-never-promised-you-a-rose-garden question"—revealing the core of new-age logic to be victim blaming.

Agatha's rejection by the family makes her desperate to assimilate to the emotional requirements of the work world. She methodically takes her regiment of antipsychotic medications and exudes enthusiasm in every

Chapter 3

---

11 Ehrenreich, *Bright Sided*, 45.

12 Eva Illouz, *Consuming the Romantic Utopia* (Berkeley: University of California Press, 1997) 201.

13 Kate Murphy, "How to Rearrange Your Post-Pandemic 'Friendscape'" *The New York Times*, June 7, 2021, https://www.nytimes.com/2021/06/01/well/family/curate-friends.html.

encounter. Although this medication and false positivity "extinguishes her pilot light," as she complains to her brother, it makes her well-suited to perform thankless emotional labor.

Luckily for Agatha, Havana's self-indulgence and insulation from the world requires that she not only have a full-time housekeeper but also what she calls a "chore whore," a personal assistant who can tend to Havana's needs and absorb her abuse. When Havana interviews Agatha, all of the film's characters become connected, creating a "map" of contemporary power relationships.

In the interview, Agatha proves herself suited to her future emotionally abusive job. As she sits in Havana's living room, she shyly bursts with enthusiasm and admiration for the actress and her home, displaying a mix of humility and outgoingness. Rather than list her qualifications, she caters to Havana's narcissism, admiring some chimes that decorate the room. In response, Havana shows off her hip spirituality by bragging that they belonged to a Tibetan monastery and that she once met the Dalai Lama, offhandedly describing him as "a very cool man." Agatha responds with wideeyed admiration and deference, even when Havana goes on to show her true unenlightened colors, complaining that her maid is absent because "one of her kids is sick. She's got like forty kids."

Havana shows no interest in Agatha's formal work skills but instead assumes an invasive intimacy and asks her about her burn scars. In response to this, Agatha performs the brave and humorous survivor to perfection with an openness to any question, no matter how personal. Agatha understands that what she is selling is not the ability to accomplish tasks, but confession and intimacy. She goes on to insist, "I would be the most loyal, the most competent, the most grateful personal assistant that you ever had," promising to be both a servant and a friend.

Havana hires her on these terms of emotional servitude. She insists that there is a cosmic connection that led Agatha to the job, since she is a burn victim and Havana's mother died in a fire. But rather than showing compassion for Agatha's condition, she parasitically absorbs her story, comparing Agatha's physical disfiguration to her own internal scars: "Agatha, I think you're beautiful. And do you know who looks just like you? Inside? Havana Segrand." This scene shows the boss as a kind of body snatcher who drains the emotions and tragedies of her employee to mythologize her own personal "growth."

When Havana hires Agatha as personal assistant, the two women unsurprisingly enter into a sadomasochistic relationship where the nature of "work" is nebulous and suffocating. At first, Havana is simply petulant and moody. But soon, as would be expected in horror, her whims escalate to abuse, showing the connection between everyday service work and horror.

One day, the ever-demanding Havana commands that Agatha move a number of heavy planters across her yard, in a scene that campily alludes to the film *Mommy Dearest*, in which a psychotically enraged Joan Crawford (played by Faye Dunaway) drags her children out in the middle of the night to cut up her rose garden. While Agatha toils outside, Havana meets with her agent, who has come to make a ghoulish announcement. Havana has been awarded the starring role in a film because the previous lead actress is mourning her dead son, Micah, who suddenly drowned. Hearing this news, Havana becomes dysphoric and euphoric at once. She returns to Agatha and takes her by the hands, forcing her to dance and sing with her, chanting cryptically: "This is for little Micah. Little miracles. Fire and water. We're fire and he's water." Agatha doesn't know who Micah is, but we can see that she has been unwillingly recruited into a death cult, and that this is just another item to add to the unpleasant responsibilities of the "chore whore."

In a later scene Havana will humiliate Agatha by giving her orders and asking her personal questions from the toilet, forcing her assistant to listen to and smell her farts as she commands her to work extra hours because "Maria can't work. One of her thousand kids has cholera or whatever." After this, she plies Agatha with questions about her sex life. Once she finds out that she is sleeping with the limo driver, Jerome, she wants details: "Do you do it with him? How much do you do? Do you come?" Physically and emotionally, Havana will not allow Agatha an ounce of privacy. In a regime of emotional labor, there is nowhere to hide.

Havana's treatment of Agatha is not simple cruelty, it is also identification. As an actress, Havana too is forced to perform emotional labor and is constantly mistreated and threatened with obsolescence. As Paolo Virno argues, workers in the entertainment industry are symbols and pioneers of a general work regime defined by abstract and intellectual labor in which "the whole person... is subdued."[14] After all, what is it that actors produce? The answer is qualities such as communication, creativity, and cognition. But these "products" can't be separated from *who we are*. Where is the boundary between the way we communicate, create, and think and *ourselves*? Virno calls these attributes "virtuosity," the ability to perform. This type of performance was originally tested out and developed in the entertainment industry, but now, he argues, is "exemplary and pervasive" in labor in general.[15] Havana—an aging, insecure actress forced to perform—is not so different from her assistant who must always be on stage, if only for her employer.

In this light, we can see Havana's cruelty as self-hatred. She has been hollowed out by her "virtuosity," and now all she has left is the power to drain her subordinates. In competing with and abusing Agatha, she can imagine a triumph over her own pain. She acts this out in her final betrayal of her employee by seducing Agatha's boyfriend, Jerome. Having hired him as a driver, she commands him to insult her assistant. When she gets him to confess that his relationship to Agatha is partially research for a script, she asks, "Would you fuck me, if I asked you to? For research? Am I better looking than her? And my skin, do I have better skin? And my holes, are my holes better?" These questions show that her seduction has nothing to do with desire, and everything to do with humiliation. In a final blow, she has sex with Jerome in front of her house, ensuring that Agatha will witness the act.

Afterwards, Havana finds Agatha silently sitting in the living room. Continuing her campaign of humiliation, she begins to berate her assistant, calling her disgusting, dirty, smelly. When she orders her to get up and take a bath, she sees that Agatha has stained her couch with menstrual blood. She erupts in anger: "Are you psychotic? I can't believe my crazy assistant just bled on my twelve-thousand-dollar couch. I don't want you in my life, you sick, fucking pig!"

Agatha declines to clean up Havana's mess, and instead picks up an awards trophy, using it to bludgeon her to death. It turns out that Havana's cruelty in combination with her father's violence has driven Agatha to flush

---

14   Paolo Virno, *A Grammar of the Multitude: For an Analysis of Contemporary Forms of Life* (Los Angeles: Semiotext(e), 2003), 41.

15   Virno, *A Grammar*, 58.

her meds, and with this she has cast off her commitments to "recovery" culture and the emotional labor of the "chore whore," unleashing her rage. Up until now, Agatha had carried out her emotional labor to perfection, always acting sweet and helpful, while accommodating even Havana's most outrageous commands. Her final act of violence liberates Agatha from these emotions, but she still does not have access to "authentic" passion. Instead, after every blow, she draws back and looks at her victim with curiosity, as if she is witnessing her own acts from the outside. Perhaps liberty, in this case, is simply the distance one needs to begin to discover a self beyond the performance of work.

Maps suggests that liberty can't be achieved by an individual, but is a collective, political transformation. As we have seen, the film links emotional labor and new-age culture with bondage. On the other hand, freedom is related to madness (Agatha's schizophrenia) and the poem "Liberty," by Paul Eluard. Throughout the film different characters recite this poem as an incantation to escape from the harsh realities of their worlds. At first, it seems to be addressed to a lover:

"On my school books / On my desk and trees / On the sand and snow/ I write your name." But finally, we find the poem is not addressed to a person, but to liberty itself: "And by the power of a word / I begin my life again / I was born to know you / To name you/Liberty." This ode to collective resistance hints that beneath the false emotions that entrap workers in their own personas, another world is possible.

The last moment of the film shows Agatha and Benjie reciting these words as they die, marking their final severance from the horrors that structured their lives as emotional workers. They have at last escaped from the crude instrumental prose of their daily lives—so full of competition, economic logic, cruelty, and humiliation. Finally, they can enter the world of this antifascist poem, written by the communist surrealist Paul Eluard, a poem that was air-dropped over France during its occupation by Nazi forces. In Agatha and Benjie's mythic death, then, there is a renewal and hope. Through a glass darkly, we see the horizon that opens when the "chore whores" of the world reject the oppressive prose of false happiness, and instead, aided by the lyricism of communist poetry, riseup against their masters.

Precarious Performances: Unplannable Lives of Emotional Laborers in *Parasite*

The pandemic year of 2020 was the great demolisher of plans and the great generator of memes. The "My Plans vs. 2020" meme was one of life's reliable consolations to those of us trying to pass the hours in front of our screens. But for many people who had already been suffering from intense precarity, 2020 was just another catastrophe in a series of events and precarious circumstances that render life unplannable. The much-memed film *Parasite*, which depicts the downfall of an aspirational working-class family, shows that the horror of failed expectations is no recent state of exception. The tragedy of failed plans is the norm.

One would expect that a world paved in dashed hopes and broken dreams would put workers in a bad mood. Yet, in a moment where success is contingent on the performance of intimacy and optimism, the reverse becomes true. The more precarity pervades people's lives, the more they double down on the emotional performances required of them. If one hopes to get a job, let alone keep it, they must not only wear an agreeable mask but also believe, or appear to believe, that mask is their own face. They must engage in what Arlie Hochschild calls "deep acting" and let themselves be guided by the obedient palpitations of their "managed heart."

The film *Parasite*, in which workers obtain jobs through their skills at self-presentation only to lose everything, reveals a condition in which precarity is directly tied to affective performance. That is, the more vulnerable workers are, the less they can afford to skimp on emotional labor. We are stuck in a cycle of "cruel optimism," as Lauren Berlant calls it, where we must invest our desires and hopes in the very system that crushes us. Says Carolyn Veldstra, "the smile is the output of the emotional labour demanded to guard against the threat of precarity, yet it also obscures its precarious underpinnings through the emotion it transmits."[16] Our smiles, then, are composed of congealed tears.

---

16 Carolyn Veldstra, "Bad Feeling at Work: Emotional Labour, Precarity, and the Affective Economy," *Cultural Studies* 34, no. 1 (2020): 4.

Without access to the comforts and "plans" that accompany stability, the family in *Parasite* must not only smile, but they must improvise a range of emotions and performances to accommodate the whims of their bosses minute by minute. Their efforts can be seen as comedic, but by veering from silliness to horror, director Bong Joon-ho shows that affective performance is not just fun and games, it is a means to destroy dreams and lives.

The film begins as a zany comedy, in which characters frantically and hilariously jump through the hoops necessary to their survival. Sianne Ngai claims this zany aesthetic is about "the 'putting to work' of affect and subjectivity for the generation of surplus value."[17] That is, zany comedy is generated by the fact that the *work* of fun is made visible, when in more conventional comedic aesthetics the labor that goes into the performance of emotions is erased. Though the Kim family are aware of their own wretchedness they derive humor and fun from ingenuity as they jury rig their lives, cobbling together the means of survival from trash and chance opportunities. Yet we are never allowed to forget the desperation behind these comic scenarios.

This humor relies on a disjunction between expectations and reality. In the neoliberal fairy tales that South Koreans are compelled to subscribe to, the Kims live in a utopia. The publicly sanctioned understanding of this world is that technology, economic development, and communication have eradicated old hierarchies and given birth to a modern society guided by horizontalism and connectivity. This myth is instantly busted by the spatiality of *Parasite*, as we are introduced to a family who literally live underground in a semi-basement that Kelly Jeong explains is a common "metaphor of poverty" in Korea.[18] As the film opens we share their eye-level view of drunks pissing on the sidewalk. As for "connectivity," the family can't afford internet service and must squat in their elevated bathroom to steal a signal from a neighbor.

Rather than horizontalism and connectivity, then, the Kims constantly find themselves compared to insects scuttling beneath the feet of the rich, scraping up their crumbs while remaining face to face with human excretions. In fact, the expression *chung*, which means insect, has become

---

17 Ngai, *Our Aesthetic Categories*, 188.

18 Kelly Y. Jeong, "Gender and Class in Parasite," *The Soft Power of the Korean Wave:* Parasite, *BTS and Drama*, edited by Youna Kim (London: Routledge, 2021).

a commonplace term in Korea compatible with the era of "Hell Joseon," a phrase developed to describe the hellish conditions of unemployment and economic precarity that beset young Koreans. Calling oneself an insect has become a wry way to poke fun at one's own hopes for upward mobility.[19]

At the beginning of the film the Kim family is certainly experiencing social mobility. However, this mobility heads in only one direction—downwards. They have plummeted from a respectable position as small business owners to taking on low-paying and degrading gig work wherever they can get it. The Kims are hired to fold pizza boxes by a young employee who herself is a precarious worker. When she arrives to collect their work, she finds that many of the boxes are incorrectly folded. She then refuses to pay the family the amount promised to them, showing that the "flexibility" of gig work includes a lack of agreed-upon wages.

In response, Ki-woo, the son of the family, manipulates her with his good looks and charm, making a flirtatious and insincere offer to apply for a more a permanent part-time job with her. She is so flustered that she ends up paying the Kims the full amount they are owed. But although Ki-woo is successful at using his skills in emotional labor to his advantage, the end result is only that the family treads water, receiving the tiny amount of money that they were promised to begin with. This foreshadows the film's entire arc. Each virtuosic performance of emotional labor seems promising at first but turns out to be an act of self-exploitation and reconciliation to immiseration.

Ki-woo's parabular journey is taken to the next level when his friend Min-hyuk recommends him as a private tutor for rich high schooler Da-hye. The recommendation itself is a testament to the disjunction between Ki-woo's lowly position and his emotional skills, as he has been able to befriend a rich college student. And with this momentum he escalates his affective performance during his interview for the position. Before she hires him, Da-hye's mother insists on observing a tutoring session. Ki-woo instinctively knows that his knowledge of the subject is not what is being evaluated. Rather, it is his charisma, attractiveness, and appeal. He has already introduced himself as "Kevin," an American name that improves his

---

19 Jeong, "Gender and Class in *Parasite*."

value by associating him with global colonial power. During the lesson, he instantly becomes a hybrid of life-coach and sex worker, grabbing Da-hye's wrist and staring intensely into her eyes. He confidently pronounces platitudes—"The heart doesn't lie. An exam is like slashing through a jungle. Lose momentum and you're finished." In a world measured by affective intensities, the answers to the test don't matter. Instead, the lesson is evacuated of content and filled back up with emotion, attitude, and allure.

Converting this emotional labor to money, the film cuts bluntly from Ki-woo's ardent performance to Ms. Park doling out bills. From this moment on she trusts Ki-woo completely, relying on his recommendations to fill other positions in the household. She imagines Ki-woo is now more than a worker, but a friend, forming a link in "a belt of trust," as she calls it. Her gullibility sets in motion the chain of events that will allow Ki-woo's whole family to procure lucrative employment, only to culminate in a final explosion of violence that reduces them to a position lower than their starting point.

Ki-woo begins by getting his sister Ki-jung (now calling herself Jessica) a job as art teacher to Da-song, the Parks' young son. Ki-jung is the slickest operator of the Kim family and after a few Google searches on art therapy, she cons the Park family into believing she is a rare and valuable commodity, extracting a high price for her services and making it appear that she is interviewing *them*.

Ki-jung's brilliance at fitting in with the upper class is an enjoyable joke but also a testament to the amount of pure bullshit that goes into emotional labor. At one point Ki-jung observes Da-song's painting and proclaims with gravitas that he will need frequent art therapy, as can be seen by the artwork's "schizophrenic zone" that signifies the boys' disturbance. "This is all a black box into Da-song's mind," she says with a mesmerizing gaze, "Would you like to open it with me?" This flourish leads Da-song's mother to open her wallet. Yet despite Ki-jung's unparalleled talent as an affective laborer her story is the most tragic in the film, as she is murdered during her final performance. This disjunct became a "My Plans/2020" meme in which her fresh-faced appearance at her interview is contrasted with the knife that is later thrust through her heart.

After Ki-jung is hired, the siblings decide to get their parents in on the action, but their quest takes a cruel turn. Whereas they were simply duping the gullible rich family up until this point, now they begin ousting their fellow working-class domestic workers. Ki-jung aims to get her father hired as the Parks' driver, but to do this the current chauffeur must be eliminated. Ki-jung accomplishes this by manipulating the Parks' unconscious sexual desire for their workers and their disgust at this hidden part of themselves, building on the connection, already established by Ki-woo, between emotional labor and sex work. Planting her panties in the back of Mr. Park's car, she only needs to wait until he finds them and constructs a vivid picture of the drug-fueled sex parties his employee has been indulging in at his own expense. In a particularly perverse gesture, he orders his wife to delicately place the panties in a plastic bag—this "evidence" clearly serving as a kinky fetish object. Although he saves the panties, he promptly fires the "immoral" driver without explanation.

Mr. Park copes with "the intimate but strangely distant relations that structure the domestic sphere," as Alby Gotby puts it, by insisting that there should be a rigid line that preserves distance between employer and employee.[20] With all of their cunning, the Kims can't get past this line or even see it. They retain faith, a "cruel optimism," that their emotional and intellectual talents will lead to upward mobility when all along their act is a futile, frantic dance performed under a glass ceiling. Even when Ki-taek has escaped his semi-basement slum and is ostensibly on the same physical level as his employer, serving as his chauffeur, there is still an invisible line between the driver's seat and the passenger seat that points to their relationship's limits. Later, the Parks' son Da-song points out the tangibility of the "line" between his family and the Kims by detecting a common smell that lurks in the servants' clothes, a smell that can't be washed out as it is the result of their dank living conditions.

Safely ensconced behind this line, the Parks can afford to be kind and supportive within limits. When the Parks no longer feel like being generous to their employees, they simply fire them. For the Kims and other

20 Alva Gotby, "Crossing the Line: Parasite and the Horrors of Bourgeois Domesticity," *Blind Field Journal*, March 16, 2020, https://blindfieldjournal.com/2020/03/16/crossing-the-line-parasite-and-the-horror-of-bourgeois-domesticity.

working-class people, however, there are no boundaries to protect them. While the Parks are afforded a neat line to protect their self-image, the Kims must contend with cruelty and antagonism stripped bare. We see this as Ki-jung guiltlessly dispenses of the Parks' former driver and this escalates as they attack the Parks' housekeeper, Moon-gwang, to secure employment for Chung-sook, the mother of the Kim family.

To accomplish this coup, the family stages an elaborate ruse where they use Moon-gwang's allergy to peaches to make it seem as if she has tuberculosis and has been hiding it from her employers. To pull this off the family must mobilize all of their performance skills. The nature of this performance is made especially evident in the cross-cutting of Ki-taek talking to Ms. Park and rehearsing his speech with his family. Here, the performative component of emotional labor is literalized as Ki-taek's speech is revealed to have been written by his slick son Ki-woo. As Ki-taek rehearses the scene at home, his son coaches him on how not to overact and to convey the subtleties of authenticity. This attention to performative detail pays off, and soon Moon-sook is banished from the Park home.

However, the Kims' lack of solidarity with other service workers has consequences. Moon-gwang returns to thwart their plans, proving that any fantasy of winning the war against precarity and immiseration is a pyrrhic victory built on the corpses of one's competitors. These undead come back to haunt the Kims in the figure of Moon-gwang and her husband Geun-sae, who has secretly lived in a cavern under the Parks' house for years as a fugitive from his creditors. In her role as housekeeper, Moon-gwang was able to care for him, but since she has been expelled from the household he has been rotting away below.

While the Parks are away, Moon-gwang returns and disrupts the Kims as they luxuriate in the beautiful house's bounty, eating the Parks' food and drinking their booze. She begs for the Kims' solidarity, but the family refuses to recognize their commonalities. They disgustedly ask Geun-sae, "How can you live in a room like this?" allowing their current fleeting luxury to lull them into forgetting that they themselves live underground in a semi-basement. Their conditioning as affective laborers lead the Kims to identify with their bosses rather than their natural allies, supporting Dan Hassler Forest's argument that "The deep tragedy that *Parasite* makes us feel is that radical love is almost impossibly hard in the time of capitalism—but that it's also the only thing that will save us."[21]

The failure of this radical love ensures that all the working-class characters in the film will enter a battle that can only end in death and destruction. The transitory nature of pleasure and success in competitive crisis capitalism is captured by another *Parasite* "MyPlans/2020" meme where the "plans" are depicted by the Kims' revelry in the Parks' home and "2020" is captured by Moon-gwang's rain-stained face as she desperately pleads to enter the house, proving that it is not only the virus that dashes our hopes but a fundamental lack of solidarity against our oppressors.

The "cruel optimism" brought on by their virtuosic abilities tethers the Kims to their servitude. But Ki-taek is finally liberated, in a sense, when he recognizes that no matter how expertly he tends to his employers' psychological needs, he will still be degraded and kept at a distance. The moment where Ki-taek experiences this humiliating freedom is when the Parks come home early from their vacation, nearly catching the Kim family in the midst of their post-party scuffle with Geun-sae and Moon-gwang. Compared to insects once again, Ki-taek, Ki-woo, and Ki-jung scuttle under the living room table while Chung-sook resumes her act as the family's housekeeper.[22] Mr. and Mrs. Park decide to sleep in the living room to watch their son, who is camping out in the back yard. This forces the family to stay prostrate under the table for hours, claustrophobically intensifying the film's spatial metaphor by showing both the intimacy and the hierarchal positions of the two families.

As the Parks lie on the sofa, just above the table, Ki-taek overhears Mr. Kim describe Ki-taek's smell, "like an old radish" or "when you boil a rag." Following this, the couple have sex, arousing themselves by talking dirty about the "cheap panties" Ki-jung left in their car. At this point, the Kims' humiliation is complete. They are objects of disgust and sexual fantasy at

21 Dan Hassler-Forest. "Bong Joon-ho: Love in the Time of Capitalism," *Los Angeles Review of Books*, May 1, 2020, https://lareviewofbooks.org/article/bong-joon-ho-love-in-the-time-of -capitalism.

22 Or rather, she again *becomes* the housekeeper. As Jason Read argues, "As much as *Parasite* is a kind of con it is a con in which the work of the illusion is virtually indistinguishable from actual work." Jason Read. "We Are All Servants: On Class and Subjectivity in *Parasite* and *Knives Out*," *Unemployed Negativity*, November 30, 2019, http://www.unemployednegativity. com/2019/11/we-are-all-servants-on-class-struggle.html.

once, supporting Jason Read's point that "in the age of service jobs and emotional labor the servant has gone from being a remnant of feudal era to the closest one can get to a universal figure of alienation."[23]

After a night crouching under his employer and absorbing his insults, Ki-taek can no longer fake friendliness. Even before the murderous events that follow, it is hard to imagine him going back to his old persona. His rage is reflected in the breaking storm that surrounds him. When Ki-taek and his kids finally escape the living room they run home, downhill all the way, through torrential rain only to find that their entire semi-basement apartment is flooded and they must spend the night on the floor of a gym with hundreds of other refugees from the storm. They are awakened in the chaotic refugee center by the phone calls of their employers, who have decided to throw a last-minute birthday party for Da-song and are insisting the Kims work through the weekend.

As Jason Read notes, the "line" Mr. Park draws between employer and employee is "fundamentally asymmetrical." While the Parks can assume that the family is always there to serve them, "the slightest hint of impropriety on the part of the Kims risks overstepping the boundaries imposed by the Parks."[24] This asymmetrical demand in the film is the source of both comedy and tragedy, as we see Mrs. Park calling Ki-jung's cell phone from her spacious walk-in closet to demand that she attend the party. Ki-jung responds professionally as she sifts through piles of dry clothes that have been donated to the flood refugees, never dropping her pleasant mask even as she has become homeless and lost all of her belongings.

It is during this stark moment of contrast when Ki-taek admits to his son that for the precariat there is no point in making plans—"Ki-woo, you know what kind of plan never fails? No plan at all.... If you make a plan life never works out that way.... And if something spins out of control, it doesn't matter.... None of it fucking matters." Here, Ki-taek predicts what the "My Plans/2020" meme has driven home for many of us. In a society that doesn't offer supports or security for its citizens, "planning" and

23 Jason Read, "We Are All Servants: On Class and Subjectivity in *Parasite* and *Knives Out*," *Unemployed Negativity*, November 30, 2019, http://www.unemployednegativity.com/2019/11/we-are-all-servants-on-class-struggle.html.

24 Read, "We Are All Servants."

class mobility are myths put forward to keep us performing our work for the profit of the few.

When Ki-taek gives up his illusory plans, he also stops performing as the agreeable and congenial servant. In another much-memed moment we see him driving Ms. Park with a bitter expression on his face as she blithely chatters in the back seat. In the film, she is rhapsodizing about the clear weather for the party, made possible by the previous night's rains. Of course, she neither knows nor cares that the same storm destroyed Ki-taek's home along with those of many others.

For Da-song's birthday party, the Parks plan a performance in which the boy will play a cowboy while Mr. Park and Ki-taek play Native Americans in full headdress. Ki-jung is to perform as a damsel in distress whom Da-song will save from the "Indians." Da-song's obsession with (a caricatured) Native American culture consistently reminds the viewer that the class antagonism in the film is not unique to Korea but a metonym of social relations under global, neocolonial capitalism. As Joon-ho said in a much-memed interview, the film reflects the fact that we all now live in a "country called capitalism."[25]

When Ki-taek refuses to enter the spirit of the "cowboys and Indians" game, Mr. Park becomes annoyed, expecting his servant's constant emotional compliance. He is finally reduced to explicitly saying what has been suppressed throughout the film, that Ki-taek's emotional labor is paid for and required and that "fun" is *work*: "You're getting paid extra. Think of this as part of your work, okay?"

---

25 The critique in the film is ruthless, but when the film proved widely popular and won the 2019 best picture Oscars award, some capitalist critics were at a loss. They had to acknowledge this profitable film existed, but how were they to explain it? For your pleasure, I include here the full quote of a writer for *Forbes* magazine, who turns the film into its opposite in his contorted description of Parasite as having a basically pro-capitalist message: "So maybe Ki-taek is wrong. Maybe it's not about refusing to make a plan because you know it'll fail— maybe it's about being okay when the plan does fail. Because rising to the top of a capitalistic system isn't easy. There's bound to be failures and shortcomings. But if you can push yourself past those moments? Pick yourself up by the bootstraps and march forward? Then you can make it in society." Travis Bean, "Capitalism Gone Wild: The Ending of *Parasite* Explained" *Forbes Magazine*, January 30, 2020, https://www.forbes.com/sites/travisbean/2020/01/30/capitalism-gone-wild-the-ending-of-parasite-explained.

Though Ki-taek still refuses to perform for his boss, this withdrawal of his emotional labor comes too late to save his family from their tragic fate. At this point, they have already accidentally killed the former housekeeper Moon-gwang and now her husband Geun-sae will take his revenge. During the Kims' final performance as servants, Geun-sae emerges from underground and smashes Ki-woo over the head, leaving him for dead. He grabs a kitchen knife and runs out onto the lawn, where he thrusts it into Ki-jung's chest. When Mr. Park reacts by recoiling from her smell Ki-taek stabs his boss, killing him, and runs off, finally retreating to the same basement where Geun-sae had been hiding for years. In his final act of insurgency, Ki-taek has broken free of his humiliating position, but, as Carolyn Veldstra argues, in our moment of neoliberal precarity, giving up emotional labor leads to an exile from social belonging altogether.[26]

In staging this ending, Joon-ho turns his film from a comic exhibition of the "zany" performances required of contemporary precarious laborers to a horror film that speaks to anti-colonial theorist Franz Fanon's understanding that only violence will purge those who have been psychologically subjugated. As in domestic Gothic works like the classic South Korean thriller *The Housemaid* and Jean Genet's play about vengeful domestic workers *The Maids*, servants rid themselves of internalized oppression through an eruptive, violent act. Not only do they kill the boss, but they also kill the "managed heart" within themselves.

The final message that the film leaves us with is that the acrobatic stunts performed all along by the Kims have served to maintain their oppression rather than giving them a chance to cross the "line" into prosperity and comfort. However, because of his deep conditioning, Ki-woo can't absorb this lesson, even after his sister is killed and his father disappears. Amidst the total ruination of his family, his heart remains subordinate, managed by the dictates of emotional labor. This is symbolized by his physical reaction to the brain surgery he must undergo after his head injury. When he finally wakes up, he can't stop laughing. He is never allowed to grieve the death and disappearance of his family members.

---

26 Veldstra, "Bad Feeling at Work," 9.

Even in his lowest moment, his body automatically performs the joviality of a servant. His heart is not his own.

Ki-woo is part of what Cho Hae-joang calls the "spec generation," a Korean word used to abbreviate specifications and meant to point to young people who spend their time chasing elusive secure employment, sacrificing liberty and free time to engage in resume-building activities.[27] With this conditioning, he can never escape the throbbing control of the managed heart. When he figures out that his father is now hiding under the home that once belonged to the Parks, he does not rebel but retreats to the fantasy of upward mobility, devising an unachievable plan to become rich and eventually buy the house. Late at night in his squalid semi-basement, he dreams of the day he and his mother move into this elegant mansion. In this reverie his father emerges from the shadowy basement and the family reunites in the sunny yard.

And yet, even as we witness this tender reunion the camera shows it through a long shot that renders the figures indistinct, revealing the whole scenario to be an impossible delusion. Ki-woo can dream of owning the house, but even in his fantasy he can't envision the exchange he will have with his family when he finally has the luxury to experience emotion free from capitalist competition and anxiety. The hazy figures drenched in far-off bucolic sunbeams remain sketchy and vague. We are left with the question of how, in a moment where intimacy and authenticity are lucrative commodities to be bought and sold, can we imagine love and intimacy that exists for ourselves, our families, our communities?

"Strong Female Lead": Refusing Emotional Labor in *I Blame Society*

A young filmmaker sits down at a meeting to discuss a script she is hoping to get produced. The male producers open with some insulting small talk and eventually reveal that they have not read the script she thinks she is there to discuss. Instead, they are hoping to get her unpaid support on some projects (written by men) with "strong female leads" about, you know,

27 Cho Hae-joang, "The Spec Generation Who Can't Say 'No': Overeducated and Underemployed Youth in Contemporary South Korea," *positions* 23, no. 3, (2015). 445.

"underrepresented voices, diversity, being an ally, how you might think people are white but they're not, intersexuality, intersectionality, breastfeeding in public..." When she wonders out loud what she is doing in the meeting if the producers already have these scripts, they respond, "We need an ally on your side... you know we just need someone like you to, like, help spearhead these projects... someone like you with a voice."

In the independent horror film *I Blame Society*, we understand that the job of emotional laborers is to sell one's "voice" while remaining truly voiceless. The protagonist, an aspiring filmmaker, tries to rebel against this monstrous unfairness, but can only do so by becoming a literal executioner of her own fate. Her transition from precarious filmmaker into a serial killer scathingly satirizes the boundaries of acceptable behavior even in the supposedly "creative arts."

The film concerns Gillian (the real name of the actor and director), a young, ambitious filmmaker searching for an innovative topic. When some friends mention that she would make a good serial killer, she decides to build a film on that premise and begins planning a documentary, *I, Murderer*, in which she will consider how she would go about a hypothetical murder spree. The film opens as she interviews her close friend Chase and proposes that his girlfriend would be a suitable murder subject. Unsurprisingly, Chase cuts off the interview and Gillian temporarily drops the project. Later, after a series of professional disappointments, such as having her script about Israel rejected because it is "too political" and being dropped by her agent, she returns to the subject and soon crosses the threshold from hypothetical to real killings.

In depicting Gillian's journey from precarious artist to serial killer, *I Blame Society* satirizes a work culture which is superficially feminist and yet leaves no room for unmandated emotions like anger or fear. Her industry is supposedly looking for women creatives and "strong female leads," but they have no use for any real transformation from the old boys' club of Hollywood. They expect Gillian to respond to rejection and insults with professionally curated coolness and resilience. Once she is hollowed out this way, though, it is a small step to sociopathy and serial killing.

Gillian is a portrait of the contradictory mandates that are placed on young workers in a moment of precarity. She must be driven and ambitious, even ruthlessly so, in the cutthroat world of Hollywood. At the same time, she, and the characters she creates must, be "likable." As she notes, she's not even sure what likable is—"maybe taking your shirt off?" But what she does know is that she has put her considerable talent and energy into becoming a filmmaker, and her student loans won't pay themselves.

Her slow build to serial killing is a response to a vampirical, sexist, precarious system that inhales the lifeblood of feminism while spitting out the hollowed corpses of actual women. Gillian knows the system is rigged but because she is dogged and persistent to a fault she refuses to give in and instead rises to the occasion, becoming a cold, calculating vampire herself. As Vicky Osterweil notes, "she is a murderous embodiment of the aggrieved girlboss, driven to sociopathic and self-justifying extremes."[28] Or as Gillian puts it, "I'm really jeopardizing my likability."

The film humorously presents the shapeshifting forms of patriarchy in a "post-feminist" moment, as we see in the depiction of her boyfriend Keith. His cloak of hipness and "male allyship" is a perfect disguise for his real work, which is gaslighting women in the film industry. We are introduced to him as he returns home from his job as an editor for a TV show, complaining about female directors who mess with perfectly good formulas by "overthinking things" and bringing in diverse characters. He "likes to think of [himself] as an ally" but rather than deal with female creativity he has the properly phallic fantasy of "jizz[ing] all over [his] computer screen so [he] can end the day."

As a running joke to frame this dynamic, Keith wears a t-shirt that says "RIP Final Cut Pro 7," an insider reference to a defunct editing program. This seems to signify Keith's identification as part of a technologically advanced brotherhood of insiders. Later Gillian will exact revenge by dressing up one of her victims in this t-shirt.

When I asked some female filmmaker friends about the significance of this shirt they mentioned that they too were in mourning for the useful program that inexplicably disappeared and forced them to change their approach to editing. "But also," said one, "the kind of person who is so deeply invested in these editing interface debates that they would wear a

---

28 Vicky Osterweil, "Seriously, It's Not Funny," *Lux Magazine* no. 2 (August 2021), 105.

t-shirt about it is maybe a particular kind of bro-y guy. I was upset when Final Cut disappeared but would not wear a t-shirt about it!" This sentiment may point to Wallace Horvat's own ambivalent relationship to the culture of expertise in the film industry. *I Blame Society* is marked by obsessive perfectionism in keeping to its own technological conceits, limiting itself to shots and coverage that could be achieved by the character Gillian's DIY documentary. While satirizing the brotherhood of Hollywood indie insiders, Wallace Horvat and her mostly female production crew flaunt their prowess in areas that typically exclude women.

Part of Gillian's emotional labor, then, is *having* talent and skills and yet still being required to absorb the dismissive attitudes of the men around her. Even though he is clearly obsessed with the technical aspects of filmmaking Keith never talks shop with Gillian. Instead, he chastises her for her shocking project while at the same time infantilizing her—"You're my little psychopath. You're my scary girl."

On the one hand, Keith's diagnosis of Gillian as a psycho is correct; but still, her hilarious parting shot captures a larger truth about this type of "male ally." As he leaves in disgust she says, "You don't believe I can do anything. And it really hurts because I believe in you. I believe you can do your elevated David Lynch graphic sci-fi novel." Keith is convinced that he is a genius while his girlfriend is a deranged hack, but this project reveals him as the personification of a certain type of cookie-cutter hipster whose grandiose dreams are simply products of a white guys' echo chamber of entitlement.

Gillian doesn't fare any better with the male "feminist" indie studio execs who want to make a film (written by a male buddy) about intersectionality, or is it intersexuality? Their constant barrage of microaggressions clearly communicate their expectations of Gillian. She is only supposed to perform the emotions of a "cool girl," someone who is attentive and flattering, and who can always "take a joke," no matter how insulting. When, she doesn't comply, they invent novel ways of dismissing and deriding her, such as offering to fix her up with a writer rather than considering her script. In fact, they have called her in to make a "look book," a way for them to advertise their own films with a feminist stamp of approval. The job appears to be unpaid.

Instead of putting her energy into this project, Gillian gets serious about her own film, in which she will become a serial killer. As murderer, she can both unfurl her creative powers and refuse emotional labor. Not only does she launch a serious "smile strike" but she uses her platform as a serial killer to expose the horrors of the contemporary landscape of emotional performance.

She starts by killing a narcissistic Instagrammer. Piercing deeply into the loneliness and despair of social media, she crafts her victim's suicide note to exhibit the materialism of Instagram culture. This does not point to an inherent shallowness of young women but rather to the emptiness that results when young people spend their lives locked into a feedback loop of competition and emotional performance. She draws a picture of her victim— an accurate one, we later learn—as someone who not only hollowed out her own life but also contributed to a spreading disease of misery and envy. In the suicide note she admits that although she "seemed so happy and perfect" she felt her insides as a "putrefying abscess ... rotting from the inside out." As ventriloquized by her murderer, the victim finally confesses to propagandizing an "image of perfection" that destroyed other women. In faking this note, Gillian tells a greater truth, that the emotional labor of self-presentation is a kind of walking death. This is even, perhaps especially, true for those who seem to "have it all."

Gillian targets victims who are complicit in upholding the standards of perfection and compliance that have ruined her own career. And we see them slaughtered alongside other archetypal villains of late capitalist rapacity. Another of Gillian's victims works for a private health insurance company. She overhears him in a restaurant explaining to his date how misunderstood he is for having to refuse healthcare to sick people, "There's a lot that people don't understand. You can't run a business like that .... It sounds bad, but I think sick people are stupid." To this Gillian simply says to the camera, "he has to die." The last thing he will hear before he is poisoned to death is Gillian's tale of being refused coverage for a minor precondition.

Gillian coolly accomplishes these killings, untroubled by the emotions of empathy and regret. Her completely deadpan performance is the logical result of a world where supposedly "feminine" traits are manipulated and degraded. Here, the only road from passivity to activity, from object to subject, is to refuse emotional compliance to the point of sociopathy. Only then can a woman take herself completely off the market.

In refusing the emotional work of *likability*, Gillian has become what Sarah Ahmed calls a "feminist killjoy" and a purveyor of what Marina Vishmidt calls "reproductive realism." Vishmidt looks to feminist art that highlights the "negativity, waste and uselessness of reproductive labour" to understand how the devaluation of this work leads to universal vulnerability and precarity.[29] The point of Gillian's refusal of emotional work is not to devalue reproductive labor but to show the end game of a society that collectively treats this labor as so much disposable trash. The end is death.

To Gillian, this death is preferable to the world offered by the "creative industry." When she brings her film to the two indie producers she met with earlier, they find it too weird and *unlikable* to consider. They take it upon themselves to mansplain what a legitimate feminist film would look like—"I just feel like all our stuff was about important female issues we talked about, like intersectionality and uh, strong female stuff, and I feel like . . . I guess this feels like a step back for women." Finally, they admit what they are really looking for, someone who can "play ball." In an interview, Wallace Horvat elaborates that Hollywood is littered with this passive aggressive type and that for her this is worse than blatant misogyny since there is no way to directly meet and combat it—"Everybody in this industry right now is looking for like, female beards to rescue them, but that's not what we're here for."[30]

Of course, this pseudo-feminism is not unique to Hollywood. Corporations and institutions are now frantic to make displays of their dedication to equality and social diversity, and as part of this project all employees are supposed to be the "cool girl" and play along, without pointing out the hypocrisy and failings of their employers. As I write this, the latest risible example is a much derided "woke" CIA commercial featuring a "cisgender millennial who has been diagnosed with generalized anxiety disorder"

29 Marina Vishmidt, "Reproductive Realism: Towards a Critical Aesthetics of Gendered Labor," Histórias Feministas seminar, 2018, Museu de Arte São Paulo.
30 Nicole Veneto, "Film Interview: Gillian Wallace Horvat on 'I Blame Society,'" *the arts fuse*, February 9, 2021, https://artsfuse.org/221795/film-interview-gillian-wallace-horvat-on-i-blame-society.

and who identifies as "intersectional." This tokenism itself involves a kind of emotional performance that transforms the language of political desire into another tool for state-sponsored serial killing. In other words, if the CIA were truly "woke" and feminist, it would stop its neo-imperialist killing campaign.

In the end, Gillian does not perform as required. Or rather she does. She apologizes: "People say right now that, like, women, you shouldn't apologize so much, you know. But I just want to say I'm sorry." As she makes her apology, she removes a pair of scissors from her purse and thrusts them into the producer's back, qualifying her apology as she stabs him over and over: "I'm sorry that I didn't do exactly what you wanted me to. I'm sorry it didn't fit your expectations. But I didn't do it for you. I did it for me." She hides behind a door, and when the second producer enters the room she lunges at him, demanding to know if now, finally, he finds her film real enough. As he begs for his life, she is merciless: "If you knew what I was, you wouldn't even ask me that." "What are you?" he asks. She responds with confidence, "I'm a strong female lead."

In this assertion, Wallace Horvat shows her confidence that people who have experienced gendered subordination through emotional labor will understand the film and the reasons why her character must be unlikable. She never tries to explain how and why her "strong female lead" is evil. She assumes that her viewer has had enough of being cooperative and tractable with employers who view women's emotional labor as a limitless resource. As Vicky Osterweil argues, this experience leads to a finely tuned sense of humor in feminists who will get the joke. To those in the know, Horvat's extremism is a refusal of an all-encompassing system of violence. The splatter of patriarchal blood is the genre-specific fun we deserve after a day of working hard for the man.[31]

In an interview, Horvat notes that the character she plays is a challenge to the complacency and complicity of reviewers and those in the industry who seek to preserve the status quo. These people in power "wanna think they're the good guys." They never want to acknowledge that women's anger is justified or that they may have contributed to that rage. In the end, this film is

31 Osterweil, "Seriously," 109.

not for those who are already enthroned in seats of power although it has the side-benefit of making them uncomfortable. Instead, it is a vicarious pleasure for those of us who are angry enough to kill but must instead smile and smile.

Unfree Girls Live: Sex Work as Work in *Cam*

Generally, sex work is seen as *different* from other forms of emotional labor— but why? The knee-jerk response to this question is that sex work is the exception to other work—it is exceptionally demeaning, exceptionally immoral, exceptionally patriarchal. However, this "common sense" about sex work's peculiarity fosters policies and ways of thinking that ultimately do not reduce the demeaning aspects of this labor but rather punish sex workers for what they do.

We saw this in recent FOSTA-SESTA legislation, which conflates all sex work with human trafficking and seeks to end both by penalizing online platforms used by sex workers. For the consensual sex workers who used these platforms, the seemingly well-meaning bill often meant that they could no longer share information about or screen clients. While the more privileged of these workers still had ways to protect themselves, the most vulnerable members of the profession were isolated, forced into the streets and exposed to increased potential harm. These and other punitive attitudes have led many feminists to recognize that labeling sex work as an *exceptionally* evil form of labor can never lead to political emancipation.

As Sophie Lewis argues, by rejecting sex work we don't reject sexism, rather we make already vulnerable people more vulnerable: "We make harlots and other 'deviants' killable." Instead, she argues, we should look to sex workers and trans people as the "epicenter of contemporary class struggle" because of their "outcast and liminal status," which denaturalizes prescribed views of labor and gender.[32] That is, as Annie McClanahan and Jon-David Settel suggest, sex work is a meaningful index of feminized labor not because there is anything particularly degrading about the work itself but because those who are "less committed to a queer, feminist Marxism" tend to openly devalue this work and this reveals a devaluation

---

32 Sophie Lewis, "Serf n' Terf: Notes on Some Bad Materialisms," *Salvage*, February 6, 2017, http://salvage.zone/in-print/serf-n-terf-notes-on-some-bad-materialisms.

of *all* precariously employed service workers.[33] Instead we must recognize with Gowri Vijayakumar that "to isolate sex work from the web of political economic relations in which it takes place is to deny the ways in which poor women and men seek economic survival, intimacy, sex, and love, in often brutal circumstances."[34]

With this view, we can sluff off the notion that the "horror" of sex work has to do with sex, and rather recognize that it is yet another example of a labor regime in which feminized activities are simultaneously monetized and devalued. That is, the problem with sex work isn't that it's sex; it's that it's work. This is the real horror. As Silvia Federici puts it, "work in a capitalist system is exploitation and there is no pleasure, pride, or creativity in being exploited."[35] Feminist theorists involved in the wages for housework movement were instrumental in recognizing that both sex work and housework are essential forms of labor that reproduce capitalism's most precious commodity, labor power— "Housework is much more than house cleaning. It is servicing the wage earners physically, emotionally, sexually, getting them ready for work day after day."[36] At the same time, these forms of work are dismissed as natural feminized activities.

The particular kind of sex work depicted in the horror film *Cam*, camming, involves performing an eroticized simulacrum of everyday life in a stylized bedroom and broadcasting live shows to viewers who can interact with and tip the model. In *Cam*, the protagonist, Alice (whose camgirl name is Lola), works for a company called Free Girls Live that sets up her account and mediates her broadcast, taking a portion of her earnings.

The opening scene shows the ambivalence of Alice's job and its relation to horror. We are first introduced to her without context in her camroom.

---

33 Annie McClanahan and Jon-David Settle, "Service Work, Sex Work, and the 'Prostitute Imaginary,'" *South Atlantic Quarterly*, 120, no. 3 (2021): 499.

34 Gowri Vijayakumar, "'There Was an Uproar': Reading *The Arcane of Reproduction* through Sex Work in India," *Viewpoint Magazine*, October 31, 2015, https://viewpointmag.com/2015/10/31/there-was-an-uproar-reading-the-arcane-of-reproduction-through-sex-work-in-india.

35 Silvia Federici, *Revolution at Point Zero: Housework, Reproduction, and Feminist Struggle* (Oakland: PM Press / Common Notions, 2012), 59.

36 Silvia Federici and Nicole Cox, "Counterplanning from the Kitchen," in *Revolution at Point Zero*, 31.

She is not nude but not quite clothed either. Instead, she is conjuring a sexy high school girlfriend, wearing nothing but a letterman's jacket, white panties, and white athletic socks. She is casual and flirty with her customers, eliciting tips for dancing around and spanking herself. After much cajoling, she pulls out a series of vibrators and tells the guys to vote on which one will "fit" her. But the vote is disrupted by an anonymous avatar who dares her to use a knife. She blocks him, but he keeps returning to the chat feed, where some of her patrons egg him on and others condemn him. Finally, he gives her a huge tip and an ultimatum, "I want you to bleed." "Fine," she says, "Is this what you want? Cuz I'll do it." She pulls out a knife and slashes her throat, slumping to the floor. After a few minutes, she raises her head and smiles, pulling bloody, prosthetic skin from her neck. With this we realize that Alice/Lola staged the whole event.

This opening scene provides clues as to why writer Isa Mazzei chose to explore her experience as a cam girl through the horror genre. In this scenario Alice/Lola is performing emotional and sexual labor, but also commenting on it. As she flirts with and panders to her customers, some are complimentary, but others are rude and menacing. Nobody crosses the line to become fully abusive, so she just has to deal with this nascent violence in order to earn her keep—as so many service workers do. But by turning her pink frilly camroom into a horror show she both satisfies her clients' lurid tastes and takes hold of the narrative. She forces them to face their violent urges and still has the last laugh. With Alice/Lola's prank we see how the horror genre provides distance from and commentary on the unspoken terrors of emotional labor.

The film turns to actual horror when Alice mysteriously finds herself locked out of her account. She goes online to find that a doppelgänger is continuing to perform live shows in her camroom. Ignored by the police and the company she works for, she is forced to take on this mysterious entity herself. Worse, she becomes reliant on the creepiest of her customers, who uses her misfortune to violate her boundaries. In a climactic faceoff, she outsmarts her rival and closes her account, but she loses the small empire of loyal fans and cultural capital she built. The end of the film finds her starting from the bottom of Free Girls Live once again, having dropped from being in the top fifty to the obscure ranking of 167,899.

Camming both exemplifies and estranges the forms of affective labor that characterize many jobs in an era where feminized service has ballooned as industrial jobs dwindle. We know abstractly that a Starbucks barista is paid to smile and flirt, but a camgirl makes this monetary relationship overt as her welcoming gestures elicit minute by minute tips. Moral purists might argue that Alice's work is fundamentally different than other forms of service labor, but this is belied by the fact that much of her work entails extending the non-sexual part of her performances, suspending her customers in a state of engaged desirous payment. Her flirty interaction with her customers' comments is the most highly sought commodity she has to offer. In this she shows the eroded boundary between "normal" affective labor and sexual labor.

For instance, her most triumphal on-the-job moment in the film is when she finally cracks the top-fifty rankings of "Free Girls Live." At the time, she is performing a show titled "Date Night" and her viewers are coaxing her to eat a steak with her hands. As they try to lure her into acting like a "barbarian," she pushes back, insisting on her classiness as she sips wine and plays Vivaldi in the background. This simple everyday behavior in which she tussles and flirts with her viewers is far from an explicit sexual act. Rather, it is a retreat from sexual explicitness. Nevertheless, this performance launches her into the top fifty, showing her work to be comparable to the ambiguously sexual flirting required in a range of social-reproduction work, such as waitressing. Dating itself, as Sophie Lewis argues, is in part a deeply privatized and individualized form of labor.[37]

With the rise of camming and "the girlfriend experience," (performing the role of girlfriend or "sugar baby" for money and/or gifts), dating and sex work now inhabit a continuum, as Maya Gonzalez and Cassandra Troyan argue. In "the girlfriend experience," they claim, affective labor provides the customer—who himself is experiencing such a deep degree of alienation that he must purchase a girlfriend—with the simulation of love, but love itself is a "pseudo-refuge from the heartlessness of modern competition,

37   Sophie Lewis, "On the Future Genealogy of the Date," *Blind Field Journal*, May 3, 2016, https://blindfieldjournal.com/2016/05/03/on-the-future-genealogy-of-the-date.

Stepford Daughters

separation and generalized dispossession."[38] The sugar baby's job draws attention to these contradictions, as she must create a natural performance of a relation that is "uncommodifiable, authentic and extra-economic." The camgirl experience is akin to the girlfriend experience, but the fact that the performer is getting paid minute by minute by a crowd of viewers exposes performance as performance when typically these workers strive for naturalism.

The difference between cam work and other forms of affective labor, then, is not so much the fact that the work becomes explicitly sexual at times but that it is always explicitly monetized. Every bite of steak Alice takes or doesn't take, every giggle, every eyelash bat, elicits payment or the withholding of payment. This payment does not take the form of wages, but of tips—the cruelest, most intimately domineering form of the wage relationship—showing the precarious nature of feminized labor. As McClanahan and Settel note, tip work—a sort of work that over half of current workers do—has historically been feminized, and this seems to be related to the fact that "tips elicited excessive feminine 'servility' and 'slavishness.'"[39]

Cam's framing shows the ways that both horror and sex work expose affective labor that usually appears as natural and organic. Early in the film, we first see Alice performing upbeat friendliness and flirtatiousness through a close-up shot that excludes the context of her performance. Then, the camera backs away to show that she is framed by her customers' data and comments. Every flash of cleavage, every eyelash bat, every sexual innuendo translates into money.

This explicitly monetized framing of Alice's work complicates her relation to the male gaze. Even though she is clearly performing sexually, we see the scene through Alice's perspective, which consistently relates her appeal to her income. The way that she can maximize her tips is by not only watching herself but watching the ways her customers are reacting, all the while keeping an eye on whether she is rising or falling in the ranks in relation to other camgirls. In the closeups, we see Alice as the male gaze is *supposed* to see her, as naturally sexy, subordinate, performing for their pleasure. But

38 Maya Gonzalez and Cassandra Troyan, "Heart of a Heartless World," *Blind Field Journal*, May 26, 2016, https://blindfieldjournal.com/2016/05/26/3-of-a-heartless-world.

39 McClanahan and Settel, "Service Work," 503.

when the camera draws back, and we see Alice see herself, this performance is *denaturalized*. Instead, we see her calculating how much money she can earn by acting as the men want her to act.

Yet even though Alice does have some control, she can't escape the fact that emotional, feminized labor does not leave the worker with any privacy. Public and private space are merged, and neither are free from the commodification. This is seen in her "bedroom," located in her actual house, which is both a domestic and commercial space. The room is carefully curated to provoke desire in the viewer, exhibiting hyper-femininity and youth with its satiny pink drapes and bedspread, scattered stuffed animals, conspicuously placed flowers and frilly rugs, deliberate romantic lighting and music. In fact, her cam room is much cozier than her actual bedroom, which has all the signs of depersonalized neglect—a mattress on the floor, tapestries hastily hung as curtains, a single picture pinned by a thumbtack. So, from the beginning her job is a blurring of domestic and workspace, what Cristina Morini calls "the new home landscape of work" where "the house and the private area become part of productive space." With the merging of public and private, and the rise of this "hybrid" space, "the decline of the separation between reproduction and production becomes even more obvious."[40]

As Robin Wood would encourage us to understand, in a horror film we must always ask what the "monster" represents, and from there we can begin to understand the political stakes of a film. While on the surface it might seem that Alice's intrusive male customers are the film's monsters, a closer analysis shows these jerks to be peripheral to a more structural terror. The "monster," in fact, is Alice's persona/avatar, which has now become detached and commodified. This literalizes a facet of emotional labor that is a kind of self-immolation. With this labor, one still inhabits their mind and their body, yet they no longer belong to themself.

Alice has developed this persona as a way to make money, but it is also derived from her own gestures, intonations, and style—her most intimate qualities. When her persona is put to "work," it becomes alienated and strange. As the film's former camgirl creator Issa Mazzei puts it, "Lola's [double] came about due to this anxiety over a [disconnect] I felt,

40 Cristina Morini, "The Feminization of Labour in Cognitive Capitalism," *Feminist Review* 87, no. 1, 2007.

over who I was online and who I was in the real world, and where that stopped and started."[41]

Emotional, feminized labor inflicts the worker with more intimate forms of exploitation than does physical labor. The worker can't retreat into the privacy of her mind or heart any more than she can find a haven away from the public in her camming bedroom. These previously private spaces and realms have been opened to public consumption and monetization. This is the monster that haunts contemporary labor, one that deftly snatches one's most intimate gestures and feelings and uses them to alien ends.

Conclusion: Down With the White Voice! Long Live the Equi-Sapian Revolution!—*Sorry to Bother You*

Like Alice, many contemporary workers are required to give up our whole selves and become absorbed in an alien persona simply to survive. But to really excel at the performance our employers demand of us, we must convince ourselves that the performance is authentic. The "deep acting" required of us forces us not to just say, but to *believe* that our suffering is our own fault, that we love our employers and customers no matter how they treat us, that an individual can succeed through pure grit despite structural inequality. And once we really get into character and convince ourselves of these untruths, then the hope for solidarity and struggle disappears along with the people we once were.

This is a theme in *Sorry to Bother You*, in which Cassius "Cash" Green experiences emotional labor as a Faustian bargain. Cash is a poor, Black Oaklander in precarious circumstances—living in a garage and on the brink of homelessness. He works as a telemarketer at RegalView, a commission-only employer where the emotional performance required is signified by their slogan: "stick to the script." Cash fails spectacularly until coworker Langston gives him the golden key, advising him to use his "white voice."

---

41 Kaitlin Reilly, "The Inspiration for Netflix's Disturbing Psychological Thriller *Cam* is a Real Cam Girl," *Refinery29*, November 16, 2018, https://www.refinery29.com/en-us/2018/11/217115/cam-writer-isa-mazzei-webcam-model-sex-work-experience.

The white voice is not just a certain set of cadences, tones, or word choices. It is a performance that envisions an idealized white supremacy. As Langston explains, the white voice entails talking as if "you don't have a care. You got your bills paid . . . breezy like 'I don't really need this.' You ain't never been fired, only laid off. . . . *What they wished they sounded like*." The white voice then requires Cash to perform a set of emotions, behaviors, and tonalities that are a form of self-erasure. He must strip himself of dignity and racial identity with every word. In every moment he performs, he is asserting to his customer and to himself that whiteness *is* success and confidence. He must demonstrate over and over that the people who are worthy of trust, of friendship, of money, of survival, of comfort—are white.

Cash finds he is exceptionally good at performing this white voice. He is so good, in fact, that he becomes RegalView's top seller. At the same time, his friends and his girlfriend, who also work for RegalView, are suffering daily from the low wages and mistreatment of their workplace. They organize a strike but Cash is so absorbed by his success that he barely participates, and soon he is whisked away from his coworkers to join the other "power callers." These top-tier salespeople are given luxurious accommodations, including a talking elevator that tells Cash, "Today is your day to dominate the world. You call the shots. You are in your sexual prime." In the heights of the company's penthouse, he is completely absorbed in his new persona, as the rules are "white voice only." Whereas below he was selling cheap encyclopedias and junk, up here he is a marketer of expensive murder—munitions and slave labor.

Every day, Cash crosses the strike's picket line, insisting to his former comrades, "my success has nothing to do with you." What was once a persona, a "white voice" that Cash put on to make money, now is a mask he can't take off. Soon, he loses friends and family. His girlfriend breaks up with him, calling him "morally emaciated." He is no longer poor in resources, but he is stripped of social support, spending his nights alone in an expensive but whitewashed, anonymous apartment.

The top client for RegalView is Worry Free, a company that entices impoverished people to sign on as slave workers for life, in exchange for dorm-like housing and amorphous food slop, and then markets their services to corporations. Worry Free seems like a far-fetched dystopian institution, but it is the next logical step in a society where jobs are low-waged and precarious while affordable housing is nearly impossible to get. In fact, the kind of labor the company offers became quite thinkable and visible where I live, in California in 2020, when hundreds of incarcerated firefighters risked their lives battling the terrifying wildfires that devoured my state. Their wage? One dollar per hour.[42]

Cash is told that he is required to attend a aparty thrown by Worry Free CEO Steve Lyft. Here, he discovers that not only must he perform "white voice" to do his job but also "Black voice," a streetwise minstrel-like persona designed to placate and entertain white people while excusing their racism. Forced to rap in front of a sea of white partygoers, he flails until he lights on the idea to just repeat the N word over and over, to which they joyously sing along.

Cash can only break from the bonds of his emotional labor and success when he encounters a creature that truly, as Marx says of the proletarian worker, "has nothing to lose but [their] chains." Worry Free is taking the next step in its campaign for slave labor by transforming workers into "equi-sapiens," a hybrid of human and horse. Steve Lyft explains that this creature will be physically superior to Homo Sapiens as well as more docile. The plan is to strip humans of their last shreds of dignity and resistance.

However, by completely dehumanizing his workers, Lyft inadvertently relinquishes the power of what Lauren Berlant calls "cruel optimism," the false hope that keeps people working against their own interests. In the end, Cash joins his equi-sapien brothers (unfortunately and symptomatically imagined as an all-male group) in refusal and insurgency against emotional labor, forced compliance, and collaboration with the enemy. The return of the repressed, in the form of a horseman revolution, proves that "low-wage work is not only the animating spirit of post-industrial capital; it is also the specter haunting it," as Annie McClanahan argues.[43]

42 Katrina Schwartz and Kevin Stark, "What's Next for Incarcerated Firefighters in California," *KQED*, November 12, 2020.

43 Annie McClanahan, "The Spirit of Capital in an Age of Deindustrailization," *Post45* no. 1, https://post45.org/2019/01introduction-the-spirit-of-capital-in-an-age-of-deindustrializa-tion.

As feminists, we may wish that director Boots Riley thought more carefully about gender in this film, but as Stepford Daughters we can still use it as a tool to imagine solidarity in the age of racialized, feminized emotional labor. If appearing human and civilized means putting on our "white voice," our "polite voice," our "conventionally feminine" voice, our "straight voice," our "cis voice," our "submissive voice," our "cheerleader for capitalism voice," our "posh voice," then let us not be human. Instead, as monsters, let's bond together and imagine how our "free voice" might sound.

CHAPTER FOUR

COMING OF RAGE: TEENS ENTERING THE FUTURELESS FUTURE IN CONTEMPORARY HORROR

The 2014 horror film *It Follows* opens in a seemingly placid, secure suburban neighborhood. All is quiet and peaceful. Birds chirp into the empty dawn streets. Suddenly, a teenage girl bursts out of a large, solid brick house. She is clearly terrified, running from something that no one else can see. Baffled, her clueless father emerges from the house, asking how he can help. The answer is that he can't. In this world, adults have no answers, but their children must indulge their fantasies of being protectors.

We will soon realize that Annie is being pursued by a slow, relentless force that plagues teen victims throughout the film. This shape-shifting monster, invisible to all except its target, never stops until it slaughters its prey or until its curse is sexually transmitted to another hapless teen. In the film's prelude, Annie decides to give up. Instead of running forever she flees to a darkened beach and calls her parents to comfort them. By morning all that is left of her is a horribly twisted and bloody corpse.

Unlike teen rom-coms that show young people conquering their fears and beginning adult lives, contemporary horror films depict young adults who have no alternatives but to become corpses or killers. In this sense today's coming of age horror films are contemporary realism, admitting that, due to dwindling access to their own social reproduction, life for millennials and zoomers is virtually futureless. The choices on offer are to bow down in front of the shrine of meritocracy and to spend the rest of one's life on a debt treadmill or to refuse, and consequently become an outlaw if not a monster.

Young people no longer expect their lives to be better than that of their parents, and they are correct in this expectation. As income inequality has grown, real wages and quality of life have diminished, making intergenerational mobility a dream deferred. The exciting, creative jobs promised by the knowledge industry have failed to appear. Instead, youths are hit especially hard by precarity, feminization, and the crisis of care described throughout this book. "Generation rent" is faced with the choice of no jobs, underpaid jobs, or what David Graeber has called "bullshit jobs," work that does not contribute meaningfully to social or psychological well-being.

Yet young women, especially, are instructed that they should be grateful for the opportunities they now have. As they huddle over their ramen, they can spend hours scanning Instagram images of social influencers who suggest that empowerment and glamor is a limitless resource. Young women are pressed to be "agentic, individualized and entrepreneurial subjects."[1] Those few who successfully "lean in" will be commodified and dangled in front of their age mates, who are told that the only reason they don't, follow in the path of these successful peers is their negative attitude or lack of grit. In this, young women "have become central figures in propagating the neoliberal dream of upward social mobility."[2] But even the young people who make it will never cross the finish line. The likely future for even neoliberalism's winners is a life of downward mobility and debt peonage.

Even as capitalism gives back less to young people, it requires more of them. As capitalism speeds up it demands, claims Malcolm Harris, a "different kind of person, one whose abilities, skills, motions and even sleep schedule are in synch with their role in the economy."[3] More and more young people are the objects of "tough love" designed to batter them into a pleasing shape for their future roles as "investments, productive machinery, human capital."[4] The generation gap does not only point to fewer prospects and downward mobility for young people, it also features a "freedom gap,"

Stepford Daughters

---

1 Kim Allen, "Top Girls Navigating Austere Times: Interrogating Youth Transitions since the 'Crisis,'" *Journal of Youth Studies*, vol. 19, no. 6, 2016, 807.

2 Allen, "Top Girls," 807.

3 Malcolm Harris, *Kids These Days: Human Capital and the Making of Millennials* (Boston: Little, Brown and Company, 2017), 5.

4 Harris, *Kids These Days*, 5.

with younger people increasingly pressured to micromanage their own identities and behaviors to fit the needs of capital.

Youths from disadvantaged backgrounds will be managed in even more punitive ways. Their "free time" will be seen as a harbinger of criminal activity, and they are likely to enter the carceral system early.[5] These are the kids that I teach, and I see first-hand the tsunami of anxiety and pressures that they face. For these kids, the "futureless future" often seems foreordained by a past that includes homelessness, abuse, deportation, and hunger. Many of my students who are only twenty years old have already been incarcerated, have had their DACA status revoked, have full-time jobs, have kids, have had cancer (probably due to the pollution in the Central Valley of California).

As a composition teacher trying to be a force of liberation in these young people's lives, I find there is nothing that reinforces the sense of a "futureless future" so much as the fantasy of individual meritocracy. Commonly taught texts like Richard Rodriguez's "Hunger of Memory"—the tale of an ambitious Latino kid who becomes a famous writer by rejecting bilingual education and assimilating into a white society—only reinforce a sense of alienation for my students. The hidden message in these "bootstraps" narratives is that young people should throw everything and everyone they know and love under the bus for a chance at an ever-receding brass ring of meritocratic success.

On the other hand, horror can be a tool to help students narrate the real conditions of their lives and to begin a journey toward realistic growth and resistance. I often teach Toni Morrison's novel *Beloved*, a ghost story about a Black woman, Sethe, who kills her own child rather than give her over to slavery. This novel does not ask the reader to strive for impossible perfection but to recognize the haunted ground on which we all walk. In response, my students' papers get deep, connecting Morrison's critical themes to their own familial histories of immigration and survival. Following Sethe's struggle to reconcile with her decision and the ghost of her dead daughter, this novel is harsh and terrifying, and yet evocative and replete with moments of determination and solidarity. With its unflinching depiction of slavery

---

5 Harris, *Kids These Days*, 6.

and resistance, it does not deny the structural horrors of our past but still recognizes the possibility for beauty and communion. This gothic tale connects students to their own history, rather than encouraging them to forget it and move on, as we see in narratives that emphasize grit and individualism. But what do I know? As J. D. Vance (whose *Hillbilly Elegy* is another terrible "bootstraps" mainstay of composition classes) judges me, I'm just a nihilistic example of the "childless left."

Even young people who have more advantages are not given time to figure out who they are and what they want. Instead, they are intimately supervised from cradle to college. As Harris notes, this lack of control gives rise to an explosion of mental health problems and a lifetime of medication. And anxiety is only heightened by youth's total immersion in the feedback loop of social media, which amplifies bad feelings and insecurities.

Yet, this "absent future," as a 2009 communique named it, also creates monsters, those who fight back. Monstrosity is in fact relative. When youths become monsters to those who demand their obedience and conformity, this resistance makes them beautiful in the eyes of their comrades. I'm no longer young myself, but I recently experienced what could be called this twofold vision of monstrosity with some young comrades as we staged a Women's Strike event that included communal childcare, free food, and beautiful painted banners that expressed our vision of autonomous social reproduction and communal luxury. We were a peaceful and utopian collective, and yet we were treated as fearful interlopers to a permitted gathering and told by cops and signs to "keep off the lawn" of a public park where we hoped to conduct our mutual-aid activities. In our eyes, we were a thing of beauty, but to those fearful of our unruly rebellion we were the big bad—Antifa, terrorists, communists, anarchists, queer, monsters. Says Jeffrey Jerome Cohen of the making of monsters, "the monster of prohibition exists to demarcate the bonds that hold together that system of relations we call culture, to call horrid attention to the borders that cannot—must not—be crossed."[6]

This "othering" is a mainstay for our culture that gives way to moral panics about young people with dependable regularity. Occupy, Women's Strikes, Black Lives Matter, and antifascist movements have been propelled

---

6 Jeffrey Jerome Cohen, "'Monster Culture' (Seven Theses)," in *The Monster Theory Reader*, ed. Jeffrey Andrew Weinstock (Minneapolis: University of Minnesota Press, 2020), 46.

by youths. Backed into the corner of a crisis capitalism and social depletion which eats its young, many young people have recognized that their only options are to fight or die.

Horror films have the capacity to do justice to these bleak yet galvanizing conditions. In horror we are given permission to explore forbidden forms of violence, and that includes both the structural violence that young people face and the inner force that must be summoned to confront these conditions. The films addressed in this chapter explore the taboo dimensions of the coming-of-age tale—that is, emerging sexuality and refusal of heteronormative roles. Further, they connect these perennial themes of adolescent experience with the futurelessness offered by late-capitalist adulthood. More, many of these narratives exemplify a trend towards "riot horror," films that mobilize the figure of the young girl warrior as a model of insurgency and rebellion.

It Follows: Now That We're Old Enough, Where the Hell Do We Go?

In *It Follows*, the viewer follows a young community-college student, Jay, whose feelings of vague futurelessness are crystalized when she sexually contracts a curse that renders her completely vulnerable. The curse is a murderous force that follows its victim, taking different personified shapes as it relentlessly pursues its goal. We gather from the introduction of the film that Jay's life up until the point where she is cursed has been a kind of lower-middle class idyll, characterized by free time and downward mobility. She lives in a neighborhood that looks like it was once a prosperous suburb of Detroit, but now is filled with unkempt yards and crumbling homes.

The setting is the first hint of the invisible, racialized narrative we will see throughout the film. The well-known tale of Detroit's deindustrialization is one of transition from a thriving center of production to a blighted place where people, especially Black people, suffer abject poverty and are deprived of even the basic requirements of social reproduction. In *It Follows*, we see the "disease" of poverty spreading and "following" the children of those who participated in the white flight to the suburbs, abandoning and demonizing those they left behind, even as they themselves can't escape the curse of futurelessness and precarity that has now transgressed racial boundaries.

Jay spends her days with her younger sister and their friends hanging out at their large but decrepit suburban home while her single mother is out working at all hours. She entertains herself by dating and seems to be going through the usual stages related to coming of age, admiring herself and preparing for sexual initiation in her still-girly bedroom. A date with Jay's new boyfriend Hugh starts out well as they lightly banter while waiting in line for a movie. But ominous music and a vague sense of dissatisfaction permeate the scene. During a silly people-watching game, Hugh reveals that he longs to be a young child, hinting at how bleak the future looks to him. He tries to guess who Jay has picked from the crowd as a figure of envy, but when he points to a girl in a yellow dress and Jay can't see her, Hugh freaks out and insists that they leave before the movie starts. He drives her to a restaurant in his big anachronistic American car, which evokes Detroit's past period of industrial thriving.

On their next date, Hugh and Jay have sex for the first time. It seems as if this will initiate Jay into a new stage of maturity, as is typical in the coming-of-age tale, but instead sex transports her into a nightmare, as she now has contracted a kind of sexually transmitted disease that can only end in horrific death. Some have interpreted the sexual nature of the curse as a sign that the film itself is a puritanical cautionary tale. In the least subtle reading I came across, it was championed, in *The Catholic World Report*, as an admonitory message against promiscuity that could have been made by Pope Paul VI himself. However, the sexual encounter that transmits "It" from Hugh to Jay is depicted ambiguously, filmed from a shadowy, neutral, distant point of view, allowing for multiple interpretations.

Although Jay's innocently decorated bedroom and child-like features code her as virginal, we find out later that she is experienced and capable of thinking of sex as "no big deal." It is not sex that defiles her, it is the bleakness of her surroundings and her future. After having sex with Hugh, she lies on her stomach, in the back seat of his car. This is the last moment of her "innocence." Hugh is about to tell her about "It," and the terror that will follow her from this moment on won't allow her any further moments of introspection. Unaware that Hugh is preparing to knock her out and tie her up, she talks to herself, thoughtlessly twisting a half-dead blade of grass:

> It's funny, I used to daydream about being old enough to go out on dates and drive around with my friends in their cars. I had this image of myself holding hands with a really cute guy, listening to the radio, driving on some pretty road, up north maybe, and the trees starting to change color. It was never about going anywhere anyway. It was just about some kind of freedom I guess. Now that we're old enough, where the hell do we go?

After this speech that reflects Jay's sense of futurelessness, Hugh chloroforms her and she wakes up to find herself tied to a wheelchair in a spookily re-greened abandoned car park. Here Hugh introduces Jay to the "rules" of her curse—the force will follow you no matter where you go. It takes different shapes, sometimes familiar forms, perhaps "just to hurt you." Only you and others who have been previously cursed can see it. You must always make sure your location has more than one exit. You should pass it on as soon as you can by having sex with someone else. All of these rules seem cruel and terrifying, and they are. They are the individualized solutions we are given to *social* problems. The underlying message is, don't try to understand or eradicate this evil, simply fend for yourself and pass it along.

To prove to Jay that she is being followed, Hugh forces her to wait for "It" to appear. Eventually, a filthy, expressionless, naked young woman lumbers toward them. It is the first of the follower's many avatars. Many of these personifications of terror show the particularly gendered way Jay experiences her fear of a futureless future. They evoke sex work, sexual assault, destitution, and homelessness. Later, another zombie-like young woman will follow her, wearing only one dirty athletic sock and showing her degradation by peeing on herself. These embodiments of the looming void that gapes before today's youth are often naked, existing in a world where all the trappings of ambition and hope are stripped away.

As Jay is learning about her doomed future, in a world away, we see her sister, Kelly, and their friends Yara and Paul playing cards on the girls' front porch. Even this state of so-called innocence, though, is haunted by death.

151

Yara has been reading Dostoevsky's *The Idiot* on a strange, shell-shaped device that serves as a sort of Kindle. She reads a line out loud to her friends: "I think that if one is faced with inevitable destruction, if a house is falling upon you, for instance, one must feel a great longing to sit down, close one's eyes, and wait, come what may." This "inevitable destruction" and feeling of hopeless passivity predicts the curse that Jay is facing, but in their innocent state (they don't know of Jay's assault yet), the group of teenagers connect it to their own anomie as drifting youth: "That's why we're drinking on the porch." We don't know much about their lives, but like many contemporary youths, they seem to be goalless and unmoored. Paul and Kelly work part time at an ice cream shop and other than that they spend their days lolling around the house in a vague state of suspended animation that we can imagine will go on indefinitely.

The crumbling house belongs to Jay and Kelly's single mom, who we only see in blurs and fragments. Her life also seems to be dominated by a low-waged job, but one that is more than full-time, as she supports her family alone and yet has no time to actually be with them. One of the many symbols of adult impotence in the film, she is not a "monster," nor callous or cruel, but she is still powerless to help her kids because she must work endlessly to keep up even the husk of a previous form of middle-class domesticity, pointing again to a world where social supports are eroded to the point of nonexistence. At several points the girls decide not to disturb or tell their mother about the horrors they are undergoing because it would only worry her: "She wakes up at 5:15. That would kill me," says Kelly, pointing to the mundane fears of the future and of what Jason Read calls "post-recession dread" that lie below the spectacle of "It."[7] Far from a symbol of cruel authority, the mother represents the teens' futurelessness, an absent presence of degraded feminized labor, no longer promising anything beyond minimal survival. The futureless future is one where even the right to basic maternal care work is forfeited.

While the teens continue bantering on the porch, Hugh's car pulls up and he dumps the half-naked Jay in the street, shouting as he screeches off "don't let it touch you." Of course, at first Jay doesn't believe that she is

---

7   Jason Read, "Liminal for Life: On *It Follows*," *Unemployed Negativity*, August 18, 2015, http://www.unemployednegativity.com/2015/08/liminal-for-life-on-it-follows.html.

cursed. She and her family take Hugh's behavior as a twisted sexual assault. But rather than elicit sympathy from the neighbors, they point out the family's declining social status, "those people are such a mess," indicating the lack of solidarity among these suburbanites who will do anything to distance themselves from the encroaching futureless future.

Where Jay was previously confident, this event erodes her self-image. We now see her looking in the mirror as a victim of sexual assault. She gingerly peeks in her panties, as if she doesn't know what she'll find there. Her body has become estranged. In a previous scene she caught the neighborhood kids spying on her while she swam, but they seemed harmless. Now their ogling takes on a menacing cast. Where before she was in a state of innocence about the threats of sexual and economic violence that surrounded her, this trauma has forced her to become hypervigilant.

. She tries to go on with her life as usual, attending a community-college English class where her teacher reads to her from T.S. Eliot's "The Love Song of J. Alfred Prufrock," a modernist poem concerning the fear of mortality. The poem, written by an upper-class white man, is often taken to be "universal." And yes, of course we all die. However, the specificity of Jay's fear is indicated by her second sighting of "It" during the reading of the poem. Woodenly walking toward the window of her classroom, "It" has now taken the form of an elderly woman in a tattered hospital gown. Far from universal, this incarnation of "mortality" is a figure of neglected old age, the demonization and desexualization of older women, and an eviscerated and anonymous health care system, again pointing to the futureless future that haunts contemporary girls, even in what is imagined as the "blossom" of their youth.

When Jay asks, "now that we're old enough, where the hell do we go?" we see that the wistful hope of adolescence is entangled with death and stagnancy in the late capitalist city. Charlie Lyne argues that the spatiality of the film is structured around Eight Mile Road, a boundary that bisects the city into rich and poor sectors, "as a metaphor for another great divide: that between childhood and adulthood." But I would reverse this claim and say that the boundary between childhood and adulthood is the metaphor, and what it signifies is the spreading exploitation in the late capitalist city. Post-sixties Detroit saw deindustrialization, joblessness, and white flight to the suburbs. Eight Mile Road is no metaphor at all, it is a concrete emblem of encroaching futurelessness.

As whites abandoned the city, it "became the home for the dispossessed, those marginalized in the housing market, in greater peril of unemployment, most subject to the vagaries of a troubled economy."[8] Black people experienced "advanced marginality" where whole populations were condemned to decaying, unsafe ruins, devoid of services or opportunity.[9] As Jon Cramer clarifies, white domination and the "successful reproduction of white communities" was dependent on the coercive and controlled "social reproduction of Black, Brown, and immigrant communities." He details how white communities drained the capacity for social reproduction in the city by appropriating and hoarding the resources needed to build urban infrastructure. But this horror of abandonment will return to haunt the suburbs.[10]

White suburbanites demonized Black city-dwellers to shore themselves up against this fate of permanent marginalization. But the real monster they face is their own complicity in generalized decay. Like the suburbs in *Poltergeist* and many other horror films, built on Indigenous graveyards, the suburbs of Detroit are built on buried Black opportunity, standing as monuments to structural, spatial racism. From the sixties to the present, attempts by Black people to transgress Detroit's racial boundaries were met with unfeeling resistance as racist neighborhood groups loudly shouted down every hope for decent housing and civil rights.[11] Instead of contributing to the city and banding together with Black people to fight a vampirical capitalist system, white people built houses with similar architecture to their former urban homes in the suburbs. But these seeming havens of domesticity were actually fortresses of racism.[12] The parents in *A Nightmare*

Stepford Daughters

---

8 Tim Strangleman, James Rhodes, and Sherry Linkon, "Introduction to Crumbling Cultures: Deindustrialization, Class, and Memory," *International Labor and Working-Class History*, Fall 2013, 13.

9 Strangleman et al., "Introduction to Crumbling," 13.

10 Jon Cramer, "Race, Class, and Social Reproduction in the Urban Present: The Case of the Detroit Water and Sewage System," *Viewpoint Magazine*, October 31, 2015, https://viewpoint-mag.com/2015/10/31/race-class-and-social-reproduction-in-the-urban-present-the-case-of-the-detroit-water-and-sewage-system.

11 Thomas J. Sugrue, "Conclusion: Crisis: Detroit and the Fate of Postindustrial America," in *The Origins of the Urban Crisis* (Princeton: Princeton University Press, 2014), 265.

12 Sugrue, "Conclusion: Crisis," 269.

on Elm Street hide their crimes from their children, and by doing so condemn the young to a waking nightmare. Likewise, we can imagine, the invisible parents in *It Follows* have galvanized the chain of death that hunts their children. And now they can only look helplessly on while their young are devoured by an evil that sometimes takes the shape of parents themselves.

This return of the repressed becomes more evident as the characters transgress the boundary between suburb and city, and we see continuity rather than contrast between the two spheres. After Jay's gang realize that she is being followed by a supernatural entity, they set out to find Hugh, who might have more information on how to fight "It." This is the first time we see the city. The camera lingers on the empty streets, burnt-out, abandoned, graffitied warehouses and homes, and overgrown shrubbery. They go to Hugh's "house" which turns out to be a squat where he had been staying in order to pass along "It" while remaining anonymous. The squat is notable for its similarity to Jay's house. It looks like a future vision of Jay and her friends' world: a large, filthy, empty husk of middle-class life.

These encounters with the futureless future galvanize Jay and her gang to fight, but by playing by "Its" rules they become complicit in the chain of cruelty that characterizes the late-capitalist city. At first, they simply drive from place to place, trying to use big gas guzzling cars to avoid their doom. When Jay realizes she can't outrun this relentless force by simply burning a hole through the ozone layer, she passes the curse along more directly, sleeping with boys and men who we know will be hunted themselves. Feigning innocence, she passes it on to her friend Greg, hoping that he can take care of himself, but even though he too passes it along, it comes back, taking the shape of his nude mother and murdering him.

As Sianne Ngai notes, the sexual transmission of the curse in *It Follows* is a "circulation of deferrals." In the logic that the characters are presented with, they must pass on their curse to the most vulnerable and abject person they can find, an "economically unproductive, figuratively kinless person," in order to protect themselves and their families from the disastrous and inevitable end point of a social structure built on debt and exploitation.[13] By keeping the chain of murder in play, Jay is playing by the "rules" set out for

13   Sianne Ngai, *Theory of the Gimmick* (Cambridge: Belknap, 2020), 166.

young people, who are told they live in a dog-eat-dog meritocracy, and that there is no way out but to participate in individualized, systemic violence.

However, the utopian kernel of this futureless future is potential solidarity. Jay, Kelly, Paul, Yara, and Greg are not completely isolated. In the course of fighting "It," they become a tight-knit group. Together they surround Jay with their care. As a kind of "brat pack," the gang seem to embody a typical coming-of-age narrative in which a group of young friends journey from innocence to experience. But the experience is not just futurelessness and hopelessness, it is also a recognition that youthful friendship may blossom into collective rebellion.

As youths become more and more marginalized in late capitalism, this also gives them a kind of power. Their aimlessness and lack of stakes in the capitalist system give them space and time to build alternate forms of sociality and struggle, as we saw in the Occupy and Black Lives Matter movements. If Jay and Kelly's mother represents the hyperexploitation of feminized workers, who are spread so tautly across all of their responsibilities that they are rendered invisible, Jay's group of supportive adolescent friends, not yet fully inserted into the system, symbolize the latent potential in these feminized formations.

We see this when the group changes tactics in their struggle against "It." Instead of the individualized solution of sleeping with people and passing the curse along, they band together and come up with a jerry-rigged battle plan that entails luring "It" into the water in order to electrify it with TVs, irons, and lamps. The use of domestic appliances is a kind of recovery project, reclaiming the tools of social reproduction to fight rather than comply with the forces that assault these youths. In this final battle, "It" takes on the shape of Jay and Kelly's dead father, and perhaps by fighting him they are directly facing the complicity of their parents in a system that leads to general ruin and lack of solidarity. Rather than pass along the curse, they explode it, as they shoot it in the head and its blood seeps out, mingling with the pool's water. With this explosive, collective victory, the group appears to have a future, but for how long we don't know. The battle against "It" will rage on so long as the structural terrors that youth face remain.

Even if the ending is ambiguous, it still redeems the many instances of care we have seen between the teens who have slept, eaten, and travelled together to protect Jay from "It" and, more importantly, believed her story that "It" is real and that she is not insane. This recognition of and struggle against an enemy that cannot be explained away by psychology or individual failure points to an acknowledgement of the real ghosts that haunt youth—the gendered neglect of social reproduction, structural racism, and economic violence.

Coming of Rage in *Assassination Nation*

The 2018 film *Assassination Nation* asks the question, why does this society want to kill its young girls? This revisioning of the Salem witch trials begins in a seemingly calm suburb, but as the camera slowly cruises past anonymous tract homes and well-maintained lawns we see that all is not as it appears. An ominous mood pervades the scene as residents turn towards the camera, displaying menacing, filmy masks. In a voiceover, eighteen-year-old Lily Colson explains that her entire town has lost their minds and are now set on killing four teenage girls. Before she tells the story of how this came about, though, she provides the audience with a series "trigger warnings," for bullying, abuse, toxic masculinity, homophobia, transphobia, guns, nationalism, racism, the male gaze, rape, sexism, and fragile male egos.

Assassination Nation's opening montage of trigger warnings lets us know that the girls in this film are not simply victims; they are self-aware third-wave feminists who have the language to describe their patriarchal, abusive world. When they call out boys for objectifying them or refusing to give them pleasure, they are not, as Bex proclaims, bitches—they are feminists. However, knowing the language of feminism cannot free them from violence. Contrary to a postmodern hope that discourse alone can change the material conditions of society, Lily and her friends must reckon with threats that go beyond language.

Having established that the girls will be hunted down by their neighbors, Lily then takes us back two weeks, to the beginning of the story. Back then, the young women were not so immediately threatened, but they still spent their days and nights navigating the perils of teen sexuality, where social media compels them to perform for the male gaze and the threat of bullying always looms. The girls dress to exhibit their freedom but are constantly censored by a society riddled with confusing rules.

Unsurprisingly, Lily and her friends rely on social media for their sense of self. But while they hope to access some sense of autonomy, the toxic sphere of cyber-sociality turns their lives into an "endless mindfuck." Much of the film shows that the community of Salem has no public life of its own. Instead, the "good people" of Salem are constantly absorbed in the spectacle of the internet. The teenagers go to parties and take drugs, but rather than be present for their hedonistic pursuits they *capture* their lives for social media. Life, then, is a kind of prison. But not only are youth incarcerated in their own images as they mediate every experience through social media, but they are unknowingly involved in a kind of *labor* that generates profit for capitalism even as it produces endless insecurity for themselves.

In 2014 activist artist Laurel Ptak created a public manifesto to counter the exploitation inherent in social media. Her call to arms was the screed, "Wages for Facebook." In it, she proclaimed that what we now call "friendship" has become "unwaged work:"

WITH EVERY LIKE, CHAT, TAG OR POKE OUR
SUBJECTIVITY TURNS THEM A PROFIT. THEY CALL IT
SHARING. WE CALL IT STEALING. WE'VE BEEN BOUND
BY THEIR TERMS OF SERVICE FAR TOO LONG—IT'S
TIME FOR OUR TERMS.

Demanding wages for participation in social media, for Ptak, was a way to demystify the fantasy that Facebook is simply a fun way to stay in touch with friends. Instead, it is a mode of control. Demanding wages for participation makes visible:

THAT OUR OPINIONS AND EMOTIONS HAVE ALL BEEN
DISTORTED FOR A SPECIFIC FUNCTION ONLINE, AND
THEN HAVE BEEN THROWN BACK AT US AS A MODEL
TO WHICH WE SHOULD ALL CONFORM IF WE WANT TO
BE ACCEPTED IN THIS SOCIETY.[14]

---

14 "Wages for Facebook," http://wagesforfacebook.com.

A tool of conformity and profit, Facebook and other forms of social media efficiently create a society that is vulnerable and serviceable to the demands of capitalism. In other words, the forms of affirmative identity promised by internet culture hide the fact that social media is a realm of social reproduction, where the time people spend is uncompensated and used to generate profit.

It is no accident that the "Wages for Facebook" manifesto was crafted in the spirit of the feminist "Wages for Housework" campaign of the 1970s. By creating this homage to a long-forgotten feminist movement, Ptak is arguing that participating in internet sociality is a lot like housework. Both activities are central to the reproduction of daily life, and yet they are not acknowledged as work. Instead, they are evidence that in order to reproduce itself, our society requires unwaged performances of *love, emotional labor and naturalized friendship.* As we see from the internet's focus on female bodies, this work is also feminized and sexualized. As Nicole Veneto notes, "The agency allotted to women in the digital sphere is largely dependent on their conformity to cultural constructions of heterosexualised femininity, demanding they be 'sexy' but not 'slutty,' 'demure' but not 'prudish.'" [15]

These contradictory demands on young women have evolved from the pressures put on housewives and other feminized workers in the home. In 1974 Silvia Federici wrote an essay titled "Wages Against Housework." This begins with the manifesto-like pronouncement: "*They say it is love. We say it is unwaged work. They call it frigidity. We call it absenteeism …*" [16] Here she is writing about the duties of the housewife, but she just as well could be talking about the emotional labor the teens of *Assassination Nation* must devote to internet sociality. She goes on to suggest that when smiles become a way that capitalism reproduces itself, the greatest weapon of the feminized worker is to refuse, "destroying the healing virtues of a smile." [17] Likewise, Ptak's "Wages for Facebook" manifesto seeks to destroy the fantasy that smiles and "likes"

---

15 Nicole Veneto, "Don't Take Your Hate Out on Me, I Just Got Here: *Assassination Nation* and Foucaultian Incitement to Discourse in the Digital Age," *Mai: Feminism & Visual Culture*, January 27, 2020, https://maifeminism.com/dont-take-your-hate-out-on-me-i-just-got-here-assassination-nation.

16 Silvia Federici, "Wages Against Housework," in *Revolution at Point Zero: Housework, Reproduction, and Feminist Struggle* (Oakland: PM Press/Common Notions, 2012), 15.

17 Federici, "Wages Against Housework," 15.

are always voluntary and "healing." Instead, the demand for these gestures of affirmation and care can become a form of servitude. Social media participation keeps us connected, but at what cost? Behind this connection is the threat that if we *disconnect* we will be unloved. Or, as Lily puts it, "the truth is, no one wants the real you. So you stop telling the truth."

Lily, Bex, Em, and Sarah use the internet to amplify their own feminist voices, but they are drowned out by a world of toxic masculinity. Their boyfriends and potential boyfriends have been inundated by porn before they ever had a real sexual experience, which teaches them little about female pleasure and much about the ways women should look, act, and respond. At a party, the girls express exasperation as boys boast about the sexual skills they have learned from porn, knowing that this will lead to future pain and humiliation. Young people sense that sex could be liberating, but they are inundated with pre-packaged images of sexuality. Their sexual awakening becomes labor as it fuels an internet economy that converts pleasure into money and data. This commodification is achieved by dividing and conquering, encouraging a culture of male supremacy and entitlement rather than a feminist sexuality that could liberate pleasure from instrumentalization.

Bex, the one trans girl in the group, is most vulnerable to the toxic masculinity that infuses all the girls' lives. She forms a mutual attraction with Diamond, a hunky football player, but the constant threat of transphobic violence keeps her from enjoying the thrill of new love. Diamond's overtures to Bex are made through late night texts, allowing him to maintain a double life where he never interacts with her in front of his peers. When they finally have sex at a school party, he is gentle and seductive. But afterwards he emphasizes that their relationship must be kept secret, signifying his shame at his own desires and driving Bex to tears. In this and other scenes, director Sam Levinson (who is also the creator of popular feminist TV show *Euphoria*) uses split screens to show how isolated the teens are, even when they sit by side.

The everyday horrors the girls face are made less nightmarish by their close friendship and their adeptness at navigating their internet-saturated world. But their tight-knit group struggles to survive in a culture with no genuine public sphere. When a hacker exposes the personal data of half the town of Salem, the girls are overwhelmed by the violent forces around them.

The placid façade of Salem drops dramatically as a homophobic "family values" politician is exposed as a cross-dresser and the high school's Black principal is pilloried by an angry white mob because he had innocent nude photos of his daughter on his phone.

The town's moral panic draws closer to the teens when Lily's older lover, who exchanges sexts with her as "Daddy," is exposed by the hacker. It is here that we see how a society with no genuine form of egalitarian participation can easily slide from the mirage of liberal democracy to an authoritarian, patriarchal nightmare. When Lily's insecure boyfriend, Mark, figures out that she is the "slut" appearing in hundreds of Daddy's nude photos, he quickly sheds his veneer of nice guy and galvanizes a genuine witch hunt to persecute the town "whore."

As more of the community's secrets are revealed, a vigilante posse forms, meant to conjure the white-supremacist mobs of the Trump era, even going so far at one point as to chant "lock her up." They waterboard a young tech geek who is under suspicion of being the Anonymous-styled hacker, forcing him to falsely accuse Lily of the crime. At the same time, Diamond's texts are revealed, and his affair with Bex is exposed. The high school football team work themselves up into a transphobic, homophobic rage, and, wearing jackets bearing the slogan "Hang 'em High," they maraud through Salem's streets, seeking to destroy the girls who threaten their masculinity.

At this point words have failed them, and the girls embrace their role as the town monsters. Huddling together, they watch a Japanese "Sukeban" or "girl boss" film that features four-tough looking women who are gearing up for battle. The young women dress in the same matching red raincoats as the women on the screen, signifying the beginning of their transformation into warriors.

But they are caught off-guard when the vengeful men of Salem invade their house with intent to kill. Lily escapes and with nowhere to go she makes her way to Daddy's house, realizing too late that he is worse than the vigilantes she is fleeing. Here, the fantasy of adult protection is completely undone as Daddy gently places her in his daughter's room, only to attempt to rape her. By feigning desire for him, she manages to escape to his bathroom where she finds his slain wife and daughter in the bathtub. At this point we see her commit to her new identity as a warrior and ready herself for battle. Etching a razor into a bar of soap she opens the door and lunges at her attacker.

Here, Lily has found what Jack Halberstam calls "a place of rage," a political space opened up by representation by and for the oppressed that marks a refusal of politeness and gradualism.[18] Halberstam argues that the depiction of violent women in film and other forms of representation has the potential to transform subjugated people's consciousness, helping to transform them into communities with the potential to "bash back," as the Queer Nation slogan goes. This imagined violence gives those who are typically threatened by domination a means to "return … the gaze" and enact a "reentry into the realm of signification" rather than identifying as passive victims.[19]

When these teenage girls become killers they manifest what Robin Wood and others have seen as key to horror's monsters. They are the return of the repressed, the "fulfillment of our nightmare wish to smash the norms that oppress us and that our moral conditioning teaches us to revere."[20] In these teen avengers we can see the seeds of what I have elsewhere called "riot horror," a representation of the possibility of collective action against intolerable conditions.[21] As Joshua Clover has contended, the riot has become a dominant form of resistance in our moment of feminized reproductive labor, deindustrialization, and economic crisis. In this context, the riot has taken precedence over the labor-centered strike that dominated an era of industrialization and production. While both strikes and riots have always been treated as threats that must be socially managed, the riot form is particularly vilified for its association with disorder and violence. But, argues Clover, it is the riot's excessiveness, when it "slides loose from the grim continuity of daily life," that signals the possibility of "social contest" in a world where it often seems impossible to break with systems of control.[22] Newly

---

18 Jack Halberstam, "Imagined Violence/Queer Violence: Representations of Rage and Resistance," *Reel Knockouts: Violent Women in Film,* edited by Neal King and Martha McCaughey (Austin: University of Texas Press 2001).

19 Halberstam, "Imagined Violence/Queer Violence."

20 Robin Wood, "An Introduction to the American Horror Film," in *On the Horror Film: Collected Essays and Reviews,* edited by Barry Keith Grant (Detroit: Wayne State University Press, 2018), 85.

21 Johanna Isaacson, "Riot Horror: Rape Revenge and Reproductive Labor in *American Mary,*" *Theory & Event 22,* no. 2 (April 2019).

22 Joshua Clover, *Riot. Strike. Riot* (London, New York: Verso, 2016), 2.

baptized in blood, Lily gives new meaning to the third-wave feminist "riot grrrl" moniker.

However, deindustrialization and precarity has also unleashed another kind of violence, that of the vigilante. After Lily escapes Daddy, she discovers his arsenal, revealing that for him, as for most of the town of Salem, suburban normality had been a mere chrysalis stage that preceded the emergence of monstrous white-supremacist MAGA/MRA butterflies. Looking back, we have seen the signs of this metamorphosis. In an opening shot, a kid on a Big Wheel bike, the perpetual sign of suburban innocence, turns to the camera only to reveal a face covered in an intimidating American flag mask, seeming to predict the fascistic violence during which Trump supporters attacked the capital on January 6, 2022.

Where the exposure of the whole town's secrets could have led to a shared sense of vulnerability, instead the fear of this precarity drives the men to purge and sacrifice the girls, now seen as demonized "others." With this behavior, the town's vigilantes exemplify the social shift we saw in the Trump era. For many, a deepened awareness of precarity did not lead to class consciousness, but rather to resentment. Toughness and austerity, as well as a rejection of pleasure and generosity, became a virtue. In response to their own "feminization," defined by lack of privacy and subjection to a precarious job market, many men sought out traditional masculinity in rhetorics of hate and exclusion. This is what Jason Read, following Alex Williams, calls "negative solidarity," a logic that fuels everything from men's rights activists to anti-immigrant sentiment.[23] Those participating in "negative solidarity" define themselves against anyone perceived to be enjoying entitlements or eluding the constraints of neoliberalism, such as single Black mothers, migrants, care workers, young women, and gay and trans people.

Operating in this logic of "negative solidarity" that targets the most vulnerable, it is no surprise that the film's football players, now dubbed the "Slay 'em High" gang, decide to culminate their misogynist mob violence with a transphobic lynching. They capture Bex and tie her to the back of

23 Jason Read, "Negative Solidarity: The Affective Economy of Austerity," *Unemployed Negativity*, October 24, 2019, http://www.unemployednegativity.com/2019/10/negative-solidarity-affective-economy.html.

a pick-up truck, in a crucifixion position. This image of Bex as the true martyr of *Assassination Nation* attests to the centrality of trans struggle to our moment of gendered oppression. Hari Nef, the trans actress who plays Bex, notes that being a young trans girl is structured by the impulse to find love while trying not to die. This desire and fear is relevant to all the girls in *Assassination Nation*, but Bex faces deeper challenges and stigma, and, because of this, represents a more radical critique of the system they face.

Only Bex understands that the hate and prejudice directed at subjugated groups is often a sign of desire. When the homophobic mayor of Salem reveals himself to be a crossdresser and has his life destroyed for it, Lily feels some sympathy for him, whereas Bex is intransigently angry—"People like me kill ourselves every day. He wouldn't mourn my death, so why the fuck should I mourn his, bitch?" Here, and in other scenes, Bex is consistently the most vocal and radical of the four girls in her critiques of rape culture, porn culture, and other injustices. This supports Jules Joanne Gleeson's claim that trans people have become central to contemporary radical social movements, not only for trans rights, but in movements against police violence, environmental destruction, poverty, and austerity.[24] The harsh conditions that transgender people endure, she argues, leads to a radical vision.

The trans experience of the family and everyday life sharpens the perception that "our conditions are beyond redemption" and structural transformation is necessary.[25] Alienation from the heteronormative family orients trans activists against conservative forces. And even as trans people are targeted for what are seen as "unproductive" desires and faced with "unrelenting disciplinary violence," this only increases the urgency to fight back.[26] As martyr and hero of *Assassination Nation*, Bex never capitulates to this violence, instead asserting by her actions and existence the utopian demand that new forms of sociality and collectivity spring up in place of the horrific, hypocritical death-drive of Salem's "family values."

As the violence against them mounts, Bex and her friends undergo their own transformation, their coming of rage. The now heavily armed Lily

---

24 Jules Joanne Gleeson, "Introduction," *Transgender Marxism*, ed. Jules Joanne Gleeson and Elle O' Rourke (London: Pluto Press, 2021), 1.
25 Gleeson, "Introduction," 3.
26 Gleeson, "Introduction," 20.

stops the cop car that carries Sarah and Em to the station, and when the officer who has been riling up Salem's lynch mob challenges her by taunting, "Little girl, what are you gonna do? Are you gonna shoot a cop? You aren't allowed to shoot a cop." Lily cocks her gun and just does that.

In the final moments of *Assassination Nation*, the young girls of Salem rise up in the name of freedom and autonomy against gangs of men who wave the flag of misogyny, homophobia, transphobia, and general repression. With this battle, it seems the future is not so futureless after all, once coming of age is seen as a collective transformation rather than an individualist dead end.

How Can a Girl Dance When She Can't Breathe?: Menace and Hope in *The Fits*

On August 6th, 2018, in Cincinnati, Ohio, an off-duty police officer tasered eleven-year-old Donesha Gowdy, accusing her of stealing groceries. Later, she described how it felt to be tased: "It hit my back real fast and then I stopped, then I fell and I was shaking and I couldn't really breathe. . . . It's just like you're passing out but you're shaking."[27] This description of being tased uncannily resonates with the paroxysms that mysteriously take hold of dancers in the 2015 film *The Fits*.

Set in the same city where Donesha was attacked, *The Fits* captures the beautiful and tortured coming of age of Toni, an eleven-year-old Black girl, alongside other girls in her dance troupe, the Lionesses. As the girls explore their hopes and fears through friendship and dance, they mysteriously fall prey to a "dancing disease," where one by one they succumb to trances and seizures, rendering them helpless as they writhe and shake on the gymnasium floor.

The story of coming of age in this community is complicated by the specific treatment that Black girls face in our moment. The hashtag #LetBlackGirlsBeGirls has sprung up as more people start to notice what has always been true—Black girls are treated like adults and robbed of their

---

27 P. R. Lockhart, "An 11-year-old girl was suspected of shoplifting groceries. So a police officer tased her," *Vox*, September 6, 2018, https://www.vox.com/2018/8/8/17665036/cincinnati-police-department-taser-11-year-old-girl-excessive-force-video.

innocence, even as they desperately need and deserve protection from the violence and hardships that surround them.

As a recent Georgetown study notes, Black girls face this "adultification bias" in every area of their lives. If they simply argue with an authority, they are more likely to be seen as antagonistic or "just plain 'bad.'"[28] In the classroom this means harsher and more frequent discipline. From the age of five years old, Black girls are more likely to be suspended, hit, strip-searched, or even violently arrested in the classroom than their white age-mates, even though they don't misbehave more frequently.[29] This often leads them into the "school-to-prison pipeline," from which it is nearly impossible to escape. Black children are regularly sent to adult correctional facilities (eighteen times more than are white children), where they are "twice as likely to be assaulted by a correctional officer, five times as likely to be sexually assaulted, and eight times as likely to commit suicide."[30]

This "adultification bias" also sexualizes Black girls, allowing them to be viewed as hypersexualized temptresses and adult women before they have had a chance to explore or understand their own sexuality, and shaming them by stigmatizing their clothes and bodies. As P. R. Lockhart argues, "Taken together, these presumptions lead to Black girls being held to a different standard and facing punishments for not fitting a specific definition of quiet, reserved femininity."[31]

As Black girls stare into this futureless future, they become aware, early, that they are unlikely to be recruited into "lean-in" corporate culture, but instead are slated to become part of the ever-growing masses of "surplus" people, who generate profit for capitalism by feeding into its cruel prison system and cycles of debt. Deprived of the idealized childhood that is mostly reserved for white kids, girls like Donesha "come of age" early as they are "adultified" by a society which strips them of the protections that shield

28 P. R. Lockhart, "A new report shows how racism and bias deny black girls their childhood," *Vox*, May 16, 2019, https://www.vox.com/identities/2019/5/16/18624683/black-girls-racism-bias-adultification-discipline-georgetown.

29 Breanna Edwards, "4 Black Middle School Girls Allegedly Strip Searched At New York State School," *Essence*, January 24, 2019, https://www.essence.com/news/black-middle-schools-girls-strip-searched/.

30 Philip Atiba Goff et al., "The Essence of Innocence: Consequences of Dehumanizing Black Children," *Journal of Personality and Social Psychology* 106, no. 4: 526.

31 Lockhart, "A new report."

Stepford Daughters

other children, leaving them exposed to violence, environmental threats, and predation.

The Fits responds to the particularity of coming-of-age narratives experienced by impoverished Black girls by exposing these cruelties. However, it also pushes against the social scripts that *dehumanize* Black girls. Honoring their interiority, *The Fits* gives time and space to the girls' creativity and subjectivity rather than fall into the brutal aesthetic language of "ruin porn."

The film begins by showing eleven-year-old Toni in a Cincinnati recreational center, as she exercises with fierce concentration. She is a tomboy and her older brother, Jermaine, who works at the rec center, is training her to box. Although she enjoys and excels at the sport, she is becoming curious about the girls' activities across the hall. Peeking into their practice room, she sees older girls, sexy and bold, practicing dance routines that showcase their grace and vitality.

Within this youth center, children and teens test their strength and skill in both boxing and dance battles, and the air is electric. But outside we can see that the city surrounding them is bleak—a stretch of unkempt lawns, freeway overpasses, and identically bare-boned, low-income housing. These exterior shots are usually devoid of people, and we learn that most of the kids have single parents or foster parents who must work full time, leaving them only the sociality of the center.

The young people inside, however, take this deprivation in stride, finding enjoyment where they can. Together, they build rich friendships and emotional lives. The boys and girls check each other out, flirt, and gossip, all while constantly pushing their bodies to new heights of skill and strength. When Jermaine catches Toni imitating the girls' dance moves, he encourages her to join them. She is afraid, but soon she makes the move and becomes a Lioness. In her first rehearsal, the older girls indoctrinate the new "crabs" with their credo of hard work and collectivity. As one older girl says to her young teammates, "stop thinking like an individual and think like a team. This is your family now." This illustrates the collectivity and brave dedication the girls show to each other, even as they are deprived of adult support.

Although Toni is a skilled athlete, her dancing in these early rehearsals is awkward and stiff. We see that, for her, the fluidity of the dance routines contrasts with her more masculine training in boxing. Beyond this, she does not fit into traditional forms of "femininity." She may be a "tomboy," but she may also be genderqueer in some yet undiscovered way, and this makes the process of coming of age feel complicated and fraught. However, this doesn't separate her from the other girls in the troupe, who are all experiencing coming of age as contradictory and frightening in their own way.

In the locker room, fragments of conversations between the girls reveal that Legs, one of the older girls who leads the team, has become impregnated by one of the boys, and will have to get an abortion. And a younger girl who Toni befriends, Beezy, is constantly picked up late by foster parents who have little time for her. At one point, when Toni and Beezy run through the darkened gym after-hours, Beezy becomes frightened and pees herself, showing that she likely has a history of the "toxic stress" that plagues so many impoverished Black girls, and that makes her easily retraumatized.[32]

In a swirl of these worries and changes, Legs is the first girl to succumb to "the fits." As the girls are rehearsing their routine, she falls to the floor, heaving and crawling, breathing heavily as if she has been attacked. Toni and the other girls look on in terror, with no idea what is happening to their teammate.

From there, many kids will undergo these "fits," which only affect the girls in the community center. These convulsions give shape to the fears that all the girls must be experiencing, as they face the prospect of leaving

---

32 As Leila Morsy and Richard Rothstein argue, "toxic stress" commonly undermines young Black girls' academic performance, physical health, and self-esteem. Some of the common causes for Black girls' frequent fear responses are: "psychological, physical, and sexual abuse; having a parent or close family member be incarcerated; witnessing domestic violence; physical or emotional neglect; family financial hardship; homelessness; exposure to neighborhood violence; discrimination; parental divorce or separation; placement in foster care or kinship care; property loss or damage from a fire or burglary; or having a family member become seriously ill or injured, be hospitalized, or die." Leila Morsy and Richard Rothstein, "Toxic Stress and Children's Outcomes," *Economic Policy Institute*, May 1, 2019, https://www.epi.org/publication/toxic-stress-and-childrens-outcomes-african-american-children-growing-up-poor-are-at-greater-risk-of-disrupted-physiological-functioning-and-depressed-academic-achievement/.

girlhood behind in a world that confronts Black women with so many threats and so few protections. However, the adults around them try to find a more concrete explanation. They assume that the water at the rec center must be tainted, causing the girls to sicken. This reflects another way that Black girls lack protection, as they are exposed to environmental racism which disproportionately affects young people.

As Jessica Trounstine argues, crises like the lead poisoning of water in Flint, Michigan disproportionately affect poor people and people of color. Because of extreme residential segregation, sedimented by two hundred years of racist zoning policies, housing policies, lending policies, and transportation policies, the "disproportionate exposure of blacks to polluted air, water, and soil" will continue to happen.[33] Jon Cramer explicitly ties this deprivation to social reproduction, noting that vulnerability is produced in urban areas by parasitic transfers of resources and infrastructure to white-majority suburbs.[34] Because of this neglect and lack of protection, Black youth often sense themselves as targets of racist genocide, as seen in a study of mostly Black youths exposed to led poisoned water in Flint. One thirteen-year-old Black girl said of Flint's leadership: "Some people are probably racist and don't care about us, because they think all (African Americans) are bad and kill people for no reason." Heartbreakingly, other kids assumed that the water was poisoned intentionally as a way to commit genocide, "cause I think they really want us to get out of Flint."[35]

Although the Lionesses consider that "the fits" could be a result of poisoning, and many stop drinking the water, they also refuse to be dehumanized by the illness. In fact, many of the girls begin to look forward to the experience as a rite of passage. In the corridors and practice rooms, they chat about their mysterious paroxysms. With the fits as a metaphor for "coming

---

33 Jessica Trounstine, "How racial segregation and political mismanagement led to Flint's shocking water crisis," *The Washington Post*, February 8, 2016, https://www.washingtonpost.com/news/monkey-cage/wp/2016/02/08/heres-the-political-history-that-led-to-flints-shocking-water-crisis.

34 Cramer, "Race, Class, and Social Reproduction."

35 Michael Muhammad et al. "'I think that's all a lie … I think it's genocide': Applying a Critical Race Praxis to Youth Perceptions of Flint Water Contamination," *Ethnicity & Disease* 28, no. 1, 2018, https://www.ncbi.nlm.nih.gov/pmc/articles/PMC6092172.

of age," the girls recognize that despite all the terrors that await them, there is also potential for autonomy and even ecstasy in this life-changing event.

In this hopeful dimension, the film focuses on the girls' rich subjectivity, not simply the terrors of their environment. Director Anna Rose Holmer was determined to honor the girls' creativity, drawing on the power and energy of a real dance troupe of non-actors whose life-circumstances echo those of the film's characters. When it came time for the girls of the Cincinnati dance troupe, Q-Kidz, to perform their "fits," they each choreographed their own version of the "dancing disease." Holmer's goal was for each performer to "explore" and decide for themselves what the fits meant.[36] Rather than seeing it as a source of pure terror, the girls enjoy the mystery of the inexplicable attacks: "Mine was serene ... peaceful," "Mine was like pop rocks," "Mine was terrifying," "It was crazy ... like I was watching it from above. Like I had two sets of eyes."

Toni, however, is more fearful of the prospect of "the fits" than the other Lionesses. For her, this "coming of age" means confronting her own ambivalence towards being a woman. At this point she accepts the label "she" but who knows what the future will bring? Throughout the film she experiments, first piercing her ears, then taking the earrings out. Later she paints her nails, only to scrape the polish off.

At moments, though, Toni finds her own hybrid form of gender expression. Midway through the film she performs this by blending the choreography of dance and boxing. She dances alone on a freeway overpass overlooking a stark lawn and a grouping of low-income housing buildings. With focused discipline, she warms up with running and jumping jacks. From there, she bursts into a dance routine. She had previously botched the moves badly when she performed them with the team, unable to conform her body to the fluidity of dance and only coming to life in moments that allowed her to exhibit her masculine-coded strength and boxing prowess. Here, though, she creates a hybrid style, performing the dance moves with a kind of androgynous grace, a mixture of curvature and angularity. She switches back and forth from fluid dance moves to powerful punching

36 Teo Bugbee, "Q&A: *The Fits* Director Anna Rose Holmer on Making a Movie about the Dancing Disease," *MTV News*, June 2, 2016, http://www.mtv.com/news/2888010/qa-the-fits-director-anna-rose-holmer-on-making-a-movie-about-the-dancing-disease.

exercises, and they somehow merge, coming into their own. Her own movements set the soundtrack in motion, a percussive clapping. Then another strain of music builds, a lone clarinet that is ecstatic and menacing at once, foreshadowing the eeriness of the fits as a phenomenon beyond clear comprehension.

By creating a horror movie that plays on the conventions of a dance movie, Holmer comments on the ideologies inherent to that genre, which generally shows a group of young people who triumph over adversity through determination and elbow grease. The Lionesses are nothing if not dedicated, but no matter how hard they work, they can't transcend the mysterious fits, showing the need for structural change rather than simple individual grit.

This can be seen in the scene where Toni finally experiences the fits herself. A typical dance movie would end triumphantly, with the troupe winning some sort of contest or giving a performance that allows Toni to find her groove and place within the team. *The Fits,* instead, effectively gives us two endings. In one, the costumed team performs a spectacular dance and Toni perfectly syncs her gestures to those of the group. In the second, the dance team experience ritualized terror as they watch Toni seized by the involuntary, dance-like spasms of the fits. This duality both points to and unravels the conventional dance coming-of-age movie, implying that the creativity and expressiveness experienced in dance does not eclipse the involuntary subjection of the Black female body to social forces beyond her control.

In Toni's final experience of the fits, she hurls her shoulders forward over and over as if in a ritual trance or a vomitous purging that seems to express a lineage of physical, cultural, and emotional pain and loss. This gesture is a window into racialized, gendered capitalism beyond the here and now, and instead registering what Nancy Fraser refers to as "an ongoing but disavowed moment of expropriation"—that is, the dehumanization and abandonment of children who are part of a generations-long legacy of forced labor and financial ruin.[37]

37 Nancy Fraser, "Expropriation and Exploitation in Racialized Capitalism: A Reply to Michael Dawson," *Critical Historical Studies* 3, no. 1, Spring 2016.

More than a statistic, Toni is shown as both a radiant individual who shines with a plentitude of inner resources and possibilities *and* as a *child* who needs protection. Her fits are terrifying but they are literally uplifting, causing her to float through the air. In its commitment to the dual tones of menace and hope, *The Fits* is an example of the potential of the horror genre to balance compassion, encouragement, and realism. Toni's rigor and potential is never denied, but neither is our collective responsibility to keep her safe.

Little Mermaid No More: Coming of Age in *The Lure*

You may not have seen the somewhat obscure 2015 film, *The Lure*, but you must. It turns out that a key weapon for feminist understanding of the "futureless future" is a Polish mermaid vampire horror musical. Who knew? The film follows the plight of two young mermaids whose anxieties and dreams resonate with fears of exile, loneliness and destitution faced by undocumented migrants and trans people. Coming of age is here historicized, as the teens' journey is contextualized within the logic of post-communist Eastern Europe, where a failing state communism has dissolved, only to be replaced with the isolation of capitalist realism, that is, the insistence that "there is no alternative" to consumerism, individualism, austerity, and precarity.

The Lure begins when two siren/mermaids are drawn to the shore of a beach town in Poland by a magnetic Peter Frampton look-alike, Mietek, who drunkenly serenades them with melodic Polish folk rock. The young mermaids return Mietek's song, promising not to eat him. But if you have to promise...

Mietek is the bassist for Figs n' Dates, the house band for a sleazy but fun cabaret, which is supposed to be reminiscent of communist-era "dancing restaurants." The band also includes a middle-aged couple who, together with Mietek, form an ersatz dysfunctional family. They incorporate the mermaids, named Silver and Golden, into their act, impressing the cabaret manager by showing him the sisters' ability to transform from beautiful, genital-less teenaged girls into mermaids with long slimy tails. The girls fascinate every man they encounter, demonstrating the duality of male fantasy, which envisions them as both vagina-less "smooth as a barbie doll" virgins *and* rank, smelly fish people.

Directed by Agnieszka Smoczynska, a young woman who herself grew up in a Polish nightclub, the film makes clear that the depiction of female "monsters" is not just a reflection of male fears and desires, but a way of fleshing out agential feminist transgression of sexual and social boundaries. Smoczynska's mermaids are an attempt to "kill Disney," as she says, instead appearing as a palimpsest of varied myths, including Hans Christian Anderson's "Little Mermaid," which focuses on female martyrdom, but also the mermaids of Homer's *Odyssey*, who are predatory temptresses.[38] The design for the mermaids was inspired by medieval mythic monsters re-imagined by a contemporary Polish artist, Aleksandra Waliszewska, who fused the image of a beautiful girl with a creature whose slimy, scaly, seven-foot-long tail was "full of mucous," and whose sexual organs are a slit at the base of a tail.[39] As David Ehrlich points out, the film literalizes male chauvinist objectification, portraying men who both lust after these young bare-breasted women and disdainfully sniff at the slits in their fishy tails.[40]

As an image of "coming of age" into womanhood, these metaphorical mermaids do not sanitize the bodily changes of puberty. They instead celebrate the excesses of the body while still pointing to the societal rejection and disgust directed at female embodiment, continuing the tradition that Erin Harrington calls "gynaehorror," horror films that reflect on our culture's repulsion at every stage of female corporeal development, from puberty and menstruation to childbirth and motherhood to post-menopausal old age.[41] This fear of female bodies and procreative functions is often accompanied by a rejection of other forms of female creativity. As Martine Mussies argues, we can compare *The Lure* to Mary Shelley's novel, *Frankenstein*, in which the

---

38 Michael Gingold, "Exclusive Interview: Director Agnieszka Smoczynska on the Allure of "The Lure," *Rue Morgue*, February 8, 2017, https://www.rue-morgue.com exclusive-interview-director-agnieszka-smoczynska-on-the-allure-of-the-lure.

39 Esther Zuckerman, "Agnieszka Smoczynska wants to "kill Disney" with her mermaid horror musical *The Lure*," *AV Club*, February 8, 2017, https://www.avclub.com/ agnieszka-smoczynska-wants-to-kill-disney-with-her-me-1798257482.

40 David Erlich, "Review: 'The Lure' Is The Best Goth Musical About Man-Eating Mermaids Ever Made," *Indiewire*, July 25, 2015, https://www.indiewire.com/2016/07/ the-lure-polish-mermaid-musical-review-1201709567.

41 Erin Harrington, *Women, Monstrosity, and Horror Film: Gynaehorror* (London: Routledge, 2019).

non-naturalness of "the monster" becomes a symbol of female artistic independence, including that of the author. In Frankenstein, she argues, the "abject identification with the Creature" is a recognition of the taboos and repressions that accompany female autonomy.[42]

Like the reclamation of the label "queer," which was originally hurled at gay people insultingly but is now a badge of pride, the celebration of the monster in feminist horror film is a way of taking back power and deflating the violence of patriarchal disgust at women's embodiment and creativity. This understanding of monstrous empowerment helps to explain the girls' attitude toward what could be an ordeal. Even though they are paraded around like trafficked prostitutes or circus freaks, they revel in their bodies and the newness of experience. We learn that they were in the process of "immigrating" from a Balkan state to the United States, but they decide to take a break and explore what cabaret life in Poland has to offer them, even though they can sense that they are being fetishized and mistreated.

When Krysia, their bandmate and maternal guide through this strange new world, takes them shopping in a local mall for splashy modern clothes, they sing of the excitement and emptiness of their capitalist initiation:

> I'm new to the city / Change what I can / change and get
> their attention / New sites all around me / The lights and
> trends / Bright shining / Buses, people, cars. We're not
> leaving. We like it / The city will tell us what it is we lack.

In fact, everyone sings all the time through this mermaid horror musical that both undermines the "bootstraps" positivity offered by traditional Hollywood movies of the musical genre and pays homage to the countercultures of eighties Poland, where glam, metal, and punk served as conduits for sexual emergence and self-realization, even as the powers of young people were largely confined to their bodies and to a few underground spaces.

The sisters handle their transition to city life in polar opposite ways. Silver immediately becomes obsessed with Mietek, spending her days pursuing a romance with him. Golden is incapable of loving anyone but her

---

42 Martine Mussies, "*Frankenstein* and *The Lure*: Border Crossing Creatures through a Feminist Lens," *Foundation* vol. 47, no. 130, 2018.

sister, and without sentimentality engages in bouts of exploration, seducing and eating who she likes. Because Golden remains a "monster," she has greater insight into the ways the girls are being exploited. She sees their new "family" for who they are, a group of sad, damaged people, incapable of love, who rely on the anesthesia of drugs and booze to function. Maternal figure Krysia and the unnamed middle-aged male drummer of the band pretend to care for the girls, but in reality these parental stand-ins are capitalist parasites, keeping all the money earned from the sisters' popular act.

Golden reacts to this exploitation with rage, lashing out by picking up a man in a bar, taking him to the beach, and eating him, then crawling back to the sea with pieces of his flesh dangling from her bloody mouth. Silver, on the other hand, responds to her precarious position by becoming increasingly meek and desperate for Mietek's love. Following the sad myth of the "Little Mermaid," she begins making inquiries about having her tail removed and replaced with human legs after Mietek rejects her advances, telling her, "to me, you'll always be a fish, an animal." Instead of reacting with proper anger, Silver falls deeper into delusional romantic love, drawing him into an abject duet with all-too-familiar lyrics that equate love with surveillance and self-annihilation:

> Come watch over me closely / Follow my every moment…
> / Tell me when something seems false / Put your hand
> deep inside me and drag me into the shore / If you do, I'll
> convert….

Instead of imagining a love that brings fulfillment and self-realization, Silver envisions a critic standing over her, commanding her, demanding conformity. And yet these servile lyrics are sung in lush, compelling tones, showing that the love song is perhaps the greatest horror genre.

While Silver drowns herself in syrupy love songs, Golden rages as a punk singer. Silver begs to be dragged to shore as Golden drowns her lovers in immolating desire, seducing a policewoman who tries to rein her in. Unlike Mietek, who is grossed out by Silver's fishiness, the lesbian cop relishes the ridges on Golden's thick, scaly tail, licking them sensually and thereby highlighting the contrast between Golden's transgressive sexual monstrosity and Silver's heteronormative assimilation.

But by continuing to live with their ersatz "nuclear family," both sisters conform, and this doesn't go well for them. One night, they present a homey scene as they gather around the TV. But a report of a murder comes on the news and the band realize that it must have been committed by one of the mermaids. At first Silver is furious with her sister, who she knows is responsible for the killing. But the violence seems to inspire the spirit of rebellion in Silver as well, and she turns on the family, demanding to know why they pretend to love the sisters but keep them virtual prisoners and steal their money. The girls have begun to realize that they are less "daughters" than trafficked migrant workers. In response, the family defends their own exploitative behavior by infantilizing their enslaved wards: "kids can't have everything they want!"

This resonates with the way contemporary youths are constantly blamed for their own immiseration. The discourse of "maturity" versus "immaturity" serves as a craven cover for the systemic exploitation of youths and other marginalized, infantilized people. In Poland, youth unemployment reached a high of 44 percent in 2003.[43] And currently young women are most deeply impacted by high youth unemployment, with many who do manage to get jobs stuck in precarious positions.[44] Due to rules that exclude people who have not been working for a long period, unemployed youth are almost never eligible for benefits and many end up leaving the country to look for work.[45] Polish based undocumented immigrants, as Silver and Golden represent, fare even worse and are vulnerable to poorly regulated work conditions and abuse. And yet, in Poland as elsewhere, mainstream political and media discourses obscure these structural cruelties with moral panics about immature and out-of-control youths. This is reflected in the ways that Silver and Golden's supposed crimes are used by the family as an excuse to treat them as disposable cash cows.

Sisterhood could have empowered Silver and Golden to rebel, but Silver breaks rank and soon resumes pining for Mietek. To win his love

---

43 Michael Polakowski, "Youth Unemployment in Poland" (Bonn: Friedrick Ebert Stiftung, 2012), 4.
44 Polakowski, "Youth Unemployment," 5, 11.
45 Polakowski, "Youth Unemployment," 17.

she vows to undergo the procedure to remove her fish tail and replace it with two human legs, as in the Little Mermaid myth. Golden makes it clear that this assimilative conversion will rob Silver of sisterhood and her voice, but Silver is too far gone to care. At this point, she will do anything for Mietek's tepid, heteronormative love.

In a gruesome back-alley surgery, Silver lies on a bed of ice and is bisected—her long glorious fish tail is replaced with relatively stumpy human legs. Though her voice leaves her as soon as the cut is made, she still sings internally, an upbeat dance tune about the promise of love and wild emotions. But her song is cut short when she and Mietek attempt sex. He has trouble penetrating her new vagina and is repulsed by the globs of blood that stick to him after his first venture. Whereas up until now Silver's surgery followed the arc of a cis woman trying to conform to conventional beauty standards, in this moment, Silver's coming of age seems to merge with a trans narrative, showing the stigma and rejection that follow when women are expected to be both "natural" *and* flawless. Even though he encouraged Silver's transition, Mietek feels entitled to his own definition of perfection, and he "clocks" Silver, eventually dumping her for a cis woman.

Luckily for Silver, she and Golden have a monster informant who advises them on surviving their "vacation" in the human world. Trident, a dehorned god who has been moonlighting as a punk singer in one of the city's seedier clubs, lets her know that she has to kill Mietek before he marries, or she will turn to foam.

At Mietek's wedding, Silver and Golden look on while the rest of the "family" try to lose themselves in lonely, frenzied dancing. Near dawn, Silver clings to Mietek for one last dance, and her vampire fangs are primed to eat him, but at the last minute she loses out against romantic sentimentality—her teeth retract and she dissolves into foam. Witnessing her sister's death, a heartbroken, enraged Golden lurches at Mietek, ripping out his throat and heart, and retreating to the sea.

In the film's final song lyrics, Golden proclaims that drifting in the cold is "so much warmer" than the frigid arms of a false lover. Although she must now roam the sea alone, Golden's final act of revenge is a call for monstrous sisterhood against the violence of "coming of age" as we know it. In this anti-fairytale we learn that to become a "real woman" is to be inducted into contemporary capitalism's horrific version of romantic love and the nuclear family. Instead of achieving this seeming "maturity," Golden opts to fully blossom into a monster who will certainly resurface to avenge herself against the world that stole her sister's voice and life.

Conclusion—*Teeth*: A Shero's Journey

Ah puberty, a time when a young girl begins to shapeshift and sprout hair, when blood leaks from her orifices and oils seethe beneath her skin's surface. With this monstrous metamorphosis comes confusion, shame, and horror.

For girls, the fear of becoming an adult is an internalization of cultural scripts that depict the female body and its excesses as abject and disgusting. But as we have seen in this chapter, it is not just a girl's body that is the object of social repulsion, but her feminized activities—her emotions, her desires, her quest for autonomy. To repress the riotous feminized desire for freedom, patriarchal logic must conquer this unmanageable creature, figured as a monster.

This authoritarian urge is satirized in the 1997 film *Starship Troopers* which shows a future earth whose culture centers around warring with alien bug creatures from another world. When this militaristic society triumphs over the enemy, dominance is cemented by shoving huge phallic prods into the bugs' mouths, which appear as explicitly anatomical vagina dentata. In this depiction of gendered fascism, director Paul Verhoeven is making explicit what most patriotic blockbusters imply: the "enemy" to US capitalist freedom is the "abject"—a feminine, dehumanized, "other." And if we don't conquer *them, they* will devour us. By using the image of vagina dentata to depict this threat, the film makes explicit that the urge to imperialist conquest stems from deeply gendered logics.

In the "coming of rage" films we have explored in this chapter, we see girls refusing to "mature" in a normative way, and rather embracing their outsider status. The 2007 film *Teeth* gets at the heart of this mythology, as it depicts a young virginal girl finding her way in the world, discoverng that for her, puberty does not just bring hair and blood, but monstrous teeth inside her vagina.

In the beginning of the film, Dawn is a devoted evangelical Christian, proud of her commitment to remain abstinent until marriage. However, she also has a deep crush on a fellow evangelical, Tobey, and can't deny her erotic attraction to him. This anti-sex culture is clearly repressive, leading Dawn to detest her own body and deny her every urge.

Soon the forces of teen hormones conquer Christ, and Dawn gives into her desire for Tobey, enjoying making out with him. But she immediately encounters another barrier to female sexuality, rape culture. Their kissing begins as something sweet and consensual, but he ignores her wishes to take it slow and tries to rape her. It is then that her secret weapon goes to work as her vagina dentata castrates her rapist.

Dawn has no way to make sense of what is happening to her body. All she can think is that she is becoming a mutant. Sleepless, she turns on horror movies late at night that always seem to feature killer crabs, evoking primordial myths of vaginal monstrosity. Soon she is researching mythology books, where she finds ancient stories in which "the hero must do battle with the woman" who is depicted in statues and paintings with huge, fanged labia. She learns from these myths that "Every man must take back the womb—the dark crucible that hatched him . . ." As with Medusa and other female mythical monsters, the story of vagina dentata is always narrated from a male point of view, as a "hero's journey" in which a rational and righteous man conquers impure and foreign feminized forces.

Dawn, however, declines to become an object to be conquered, instead experiencing a "shero's journey" during which she learns that it is not she, but the forces of patriarchy and environmental pollution, that are her town's demons. Her vagina dentata, on the other hand, is not a curse but a *weapon* for feminism. It turns out that this protective excrescence only attacks when she is raped. She can, after all, have a fulfilling sex life, if she can ever find a boy or man who will see her as more than a piece of meat. In the meantime, she can take possession of her body, clamping down on whoever would dare violate her autonomy. Even her virginal persona becomes a weapon as she dons a pure white gown and seduces her stepbrother, who molested her as a child and let her mother die. After confidently luring him in, Dawn castrates him and, as a final humiliation, feeds his offending member to the aggressive dog he has trained to intimidate women.

In the campy "riot horror" of *Teeth* and the other films I have explored in this chapter, girls learn to cast aside their social conditioning to be passive and pliant. Rather than give in to the myths that frame female sexuality and autonomy as polluted and stained, these girls learn to embrace these monstrous archetypes and turn them against the forces that would repress them. Dawn's "coming of rage" erupts when she realizes her vagina dentata is not a deformity but a gift. The gynecologist who rapes her loses some fingers and her next rapist is succinctly castrated as well. Soon, she understands that she has options, she can move through the world, and anyone who tries to mess with her won't live to regret it. Like the other young sheroes of horror, Dawn will not capitulate to the sanctioned model of womanhood. Instead, she will transform into a monster who knows what she wants and knows how to bite back.

CODA

BECOMING MONSTER

Many of my feminist friends are more disturbed than excited at the thought of watching a horror film. It's often hard to explain my exuberance when I have a free evening to binge on my favorite genre. And it's probably tough for them to reconcile my (hopefully not too annoyingly) cheerful personality with this seemingly morbid interest. More than once I have asked myself why I don't prefer positive films. Why not spend my time with narratives that offer a blueprint for a feminist anticapitalist future? The Marxist critic Fredric Jameson offered one answer when he argued that representations of utopia are necessarily myopic. We might think that we are sketching out the future, but we are actually limiting our vision, since all we have to work with are the possibilities we can imagine in the present. In horror we can experience the pleasure of a refusal that is uncompromising. We don't have to respect the limits of "practicality" or "maturity." We can be excessive, leaping over the bureaucrats who mete out hope in tiny portions. We can blaspheme against the widespread reverence for bland, technocratic, incremental "progress."

Another reason for my love of horror could just be luck. While many women's first encounter with the genre was harrowing and misogynist, I happened across a rare feminist classic. When I was seven years old, I saw the "Talky Tina" episode of *The Twilight Zone*, not a show generally known for its feminist themes. However, not only was this my first experience of watching horror, but probably my introduction to feminism. In the episode, a sadistic stepfather meets his match in his stepdaughter's seemingly innocuous doll. It is made clear that this man's wife and child are completely dependent on him, financially and emotionally. This makes them helpless against his abuse. But once the animated Tina doll arrives on the scene, she fearlessly tells him she hates him. And later, even though she is only a tiny, frail doll, she will make good on a threat to kill him. In no other scenario than one dreamt up by the horror genre can we imagine the two women in that household escaping from under their master's thumb. The avenging Tina doll gives voice to the voiceless, power to the powerless.

The films I have explored in this book largely continue the tradition of "Talky Tina," helping us imagine feminist rage and vengeance. But even when horror is not explicit about its message, we can still gain weapons for rebellion, as we develop our critical skills to read against the grain.

As I hope this book has proved, the negation found in horror need not be seen as nihilistic. It can be a way of undoing the myths that confine us, and by doing so freeing up space to imagine alternatives. As an example of negation as *hope*, I often return to the Marxist critic Walter Benjamin's critique of progress in his essay "On the Concept of History." Progress sounds like a great thing. How can anyone be against it? But progress is the word that is used to justify some of our greatest evils—the stealing of Indigenous land, the enslavement of millions of Black people, the development of weaponry capable of mass destruction. This progress will end up killing Benjamin, a Jew who committed suicide rather than let himself be captured by the Nazis who hounded him in their own demented quest for "progress."

In his essay, Benjamin imagines a horror scenario. We see a catastrophic angel—"His eyes are staring, his mouth is open, his wings are spread. . . . His face is turned toward the past."[1] This fantastic being refuses to look hopefully into the sunny pre-planned future, and instead peers backwards into history, casting his gaze toward the dead. But, as in a horror film, in looking toward death and destruction, this figure is performing an act of resurrection. These reanimated corpses are the martyrs of history, those who struggled for freedom and collectivity, but who were mowed down by the forces of progress. These zombie heroes will arise and stalk the earth when "empty homogeneous time" finally stops and the revolution against ruinous progress erupts, tearing through the fabric of history.

1 Walter Benjamin, "Theses on the Philosophy of History," in *Illuminations*, ed. Hannah Arendt (Boston: Houghton Mifflin Harcourt, 1968), 257.

Monsters conjure the "undead" that our rulers seek to vilify—the communist, Indigenous, enslaved, feminist insurgents who may have been slaughtered by the "winners" of history, but whose struggles will not stay underground, so long as we keep digging them up. For those who want to protect the status quo, these undead zombies may look like monsters, but to us and to Benjamin their monstrosity holds a kind of beauty. These are both our ancestors and our futurity, the remnants of the fighting spirit that is resurrected in every moment of collective resistance.

The undead call from the past and the future, disrupting the staid "triumphal procession" of the ruling classes with their blockbusters that celebrate patriotic warfare and sentimental heteronormativity. With Benjamin, we insist that "there never has been a document of culture which is not simultaneously one of barbarism."[2] By honoring monsters, we honor disruption, we refuse to quietly follow the parade of oppressors who demand our compliance and who insist their continued victory is inevitable.

Enjoying horror and using it as a weapon for anti-capitalist feminism is a process of "becoming monster," retooling our own consciousness. As monsters, we identify with the ghosts that disturb our bland, celebratory cultural narratives. We may appear terrifying, but that is only because change is scary. As monsters, we know we must fight for social transformation, even though this will make us hideous in the eyes of some. Becoming monster is a gesture of hope, a divestment from bootstraps narratives of improvement, meritocracy, and leaning in. Becoming monster is an embrace of the "abject" qualities labeled "feminine." It is a rebellion from masculine rationalization of the world as it is. It is an attack on the thrusting, transactional, bellicose machinations of capitalist progress.

The logic of progress demands that we instrumentalize all our best qualities—our love, our gentleness, our resilience, our wildness. Capitalist logic forces us to turn these qualities into commodities, refine them and blunt them to accommodate the needs of our current

---

2 Benjamin, "Theses on the Philosophy of History," 256.

regimes of service labor, flexible labor, creative labor, emotional labor, reproductive labor, care labor and the rest of it.

· By embracing the abject and becoming monster, we become Mary from *American Mary*, who conquers student loans and rapists alike with her sharpened scalpel. We become Esther from *In My Skin*, who drops out of the yuppie rat race to feast deliciously on her own skin. We become Anna from *Bad Hair*, who battles against a vampiric hair weave, revealing the death cult of white supremacist beauty standards. We become Laura from *Unfriended*, who returns from the dead to subsume the panopticon of social media and destroy its bullies. We become Tina from *Border*, who learns to live as an intersex troll, finding dignity in being "inhuman." We become Aila from *Rhymes for Young Ghouls*, who extracts gore-spattered payback from the Indian residential school that stole her parents' childhoods. We become Ava from *Ex Machina*, who beats tech-bro incels and alphas at their own games. We become Jen from *Revenge*, who is baptized in her own blood, transforming from a boy-toy to an anti-misogynist warrior. We become Red from *Us*, an avenger of the global underworld whose lifeblood is cruelly and invisibly drained to support the lifestyle of middle-class families in the US. We become Grace from *Ready or Not*, who reduces the classist, misogynist institution of marriage to ash, along with her shredded wedding dress. We become Susie from *Suspiria*, who is transfigured from meek, beaten-down country girl to the queen of an anti-fascist witch cult. We become Ginger from *Ginger Snaps* and Jennifer from *Jennifer's Body*, who refuse to be devoured by the objectifying male gaze and instead feast on their would-be predators.[3]

The most important weapons offered in this book have nothing to do with watching movies. Rather, they are weapons of defense against the gaslighting forces that would frame our most beautiful gestures as monstrous. In becoming monster, we consider what reproductive labor might look like if we did it for ourselves. We reimagine care as what Kathi Weeks calls "collective autonomy" rather than an "ethic of work."[4] We can, with Paulo Virno, understand that negation and the refusal of work is not simply saying no,

---

3 Tragically, there wasn't room to include many cherished films in this book, but this is a little addendum to check out!

4 Kathi Weeks, *The Problem with Work*, (Durham: Duke University Press, 2011), 168.

it is a recognition of our own capacities and "latent wealth, an abundance of possibilities."[5] We join in women's strikes and mutual-aid projects. We refuse to smile on demand and to be placidly date raped. We fight for clean air and safe places to live. We refuse jails and police brutality. As in *False Positive*, we suckle a mutant baby girl that a history of systemic, rationalized misogyny tried to euthanize. As we turn to our rulers, covered in blood, a mutant child at our breast, we appear as grotesque abominations, but this is only because our beauty and care is no longer for them. We are monsters for each other.

Coda

5   Paolo Virno, "Virtuosity and Revolution: The Poltical Theory of Exodus," in *Radical Thought in Italy: A Potential Politics*, edited by Paolo Virno and Michael Hardt (Minneapolis: University of Minnesota Press, 1996), 199.

ABOUT THE AUTHOR

Johanna Isaacson writes academic and popular pieces on horror and politics. She is a professor of English at Modesto Junior College and a founding editor of *Blind Field Journal*. She is the author of *The Ballerina and the Bull*, has published widely in academic and popular journals, and runs the Facebook group "Anti-capitalist Feminists Who Like Horror Films."

ABOUT COMMON NOTIONS

Common Notions is a publishing house and programming platform that fosters new formulations of living autonomy. We aim to circulate timely reflections, clear critiques, and inspiring strategies that amplify movements for social justice.

Our publications trace a constellation of critical and visionary meditations on the organization of freedom. By any media necessary, we seek to nourish the imagination and generalize common notions about the creation of other worlds beyond state and capital. Inspired by various traditions of autonomism and liberation—in the US and internationally, historical and emerging from contemporary movements—our publications provide resources for a collective reading of struggles past, present, and to come.

Common Notions regularly collaborates with political collectives, militant authors, radical presses, and maverick designers around the world. Our political and aesthetic pursuits are dreamed and realized with Antumbra Designs.

www.commonnotions.org
info@commonnotions.org

MORE FROM COMMON NOTIONS

Comedy Against Work: Utopian Longing in Dystopian Times

By Madeline Lane-McKinley

978-1-942173-70-0
$20
256 pages

When work is slowly killing us and destroying the planet and, at the same time, something impossible to imagine life without, Lane-McKinley considers the possibility of comedy as a revolutionary practice. By appealing to laughter—what Walter Benjamin called the most "revolutionary emotion of the masses," or as Audre Lorde put it, the "open and fearless underlining" of our capacity for joy—we can counteract many of our shared miseries under capitalism, including our relationship to work.

But to think through these revolutionary aspects of comedy as a practice also involves troubling comedy's relationship to the global right turn of the last decade. Stand-up comedy's claims to the artistic freedom of hate speech in comedy represent a fascistic current of our world today, blurring the boundaries between left and "alt" right. Against this current, *Comedy Against Work* draws from a tradition of feminist critical utopianism, Marxist-feminism, and contemporary cultural criticism to reflect on an anti-fascist poetics of comedy, grounded in a critique of work.

MORE FROM COMMON NOTIONS

The Feminist Subversion of the Economy: Contributions for Life Against Capital

By Amaia Pérez Orozco
Translated by Liz Mason-Deese

978-1-942173-19-9
$22
288 pages

In the face of unending economic crises and climate catastrophe, we must consider, *what does a dignified life look like?* Feminist intellectual and activist Amaia Pérez Orozco powerfully and provocatively outlines a vision for a web of life sustained collectively with care, mutualism, and in balance with our ecological world. That vision is a call to action to subvert the foundational order of racial capitalism, colonial violence, and a heteropatriarchal economy that threatens every form of life.

The Feminist Subversion of the Economy makes the connection between the systems that promise more devastation and destruction of life in the name of profit—and rallies women, LGBTQ+ communities, and movements worldwide to center gender and social reproduction in a vision for a balanced ecology, a just economy, and a free society.

Newly translated and updated in collaboration with Liz Mason-Deese.

BECOME A MONTHLY SUSTAINER

These are decisive times, ripe with challenges and possibility, heartache and beautiful inspiration. More than ever, we need timely reflections, clear critiques, and inspiring strategies that can help movements for social justice grow and transform society.

Help us amplify those necessary words, deeds, and dreams that our liberation movements and our worlds so urgently need.

Movements are sustained by people like you, whose fugitive words, deeds, and dreams bend against the world of domination and exploitation.

For collective imagination, dedicated practices of love and study, and organized acts of freedom.

By any media necessary.
With your love and support.

Monthly sustainers start at $12 and $25.

Join us at commonnotions.org/sustain.